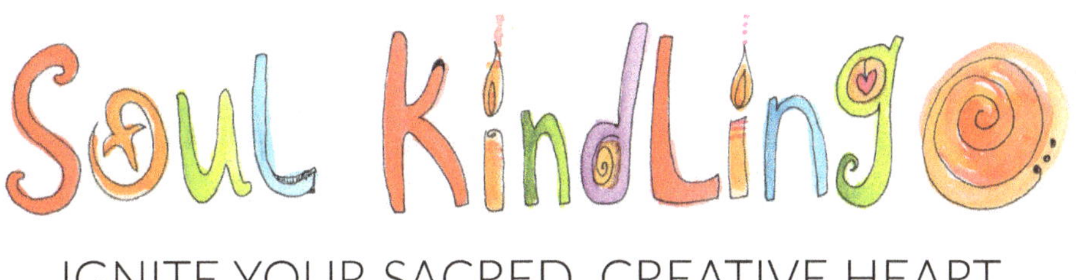

Soul Kindling

IGNITE YOUR SACRED, CREATIVE HEART

Ally Markotich

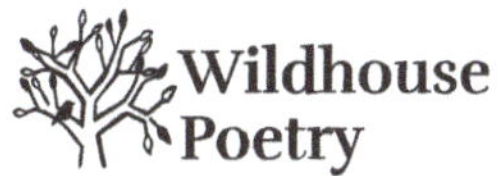
Wildhouse Poetry

Design by Melody Stanford Martin

Published by Wildhouse Poetry, an imprint of Wildhouse Publishing (www. wildhousepublishing.com). No part of this book may be reproduced in any manner without the written permission from the publisher, except in brief quotations embodied in critical articles or reviews. Contact info@ wildhousepublishing.com.

Printed in the USA

ISBN: 978-1-961741-15-7

Praise for Soul Kindling

"In these complex and often heavy times, we can all benefit from some kindling for our souls. Ally delivers this spark generously through playful image and dancing words. Each page offers its own portal of inspiration so that you too might find your vision expanding. Through practices of loosening, gazing, slowing, being, unfolding, she invites us to enter a space of holy birthing, where the new can come alive through us in beautiful ways." — Christine Valters Paintner, PhD, online abbess of AbbeyoftheArts.com and author of *The Wisdom of Wild Grace: Poems* and *The Love of Thousands: How Angels, Saints, and Ancestors Walk with Us toward Holiness*

"Ah! What a delight to experience this book. I say 'experience' because you can feel the veils of disconnection dropping as you resonate with Ally Markotich's delicious words. Right from the start, you can feel the heart of a soulful woman speaking directly to you. Markotich speaks wisdom in gentle strokes so that you too can embody the creativity, soulful spirituality, and earth-centric relationship with life you may have forgotten you already have." — Victoria Loorz, author of *Church of the Wild: How Nature Invites Us into the Sacred* and founder/director of the Center for Wild Spirituality

"Ally Markotich's *Soul Kindling* is a feast for the eyes and a blessing for the heart; it combines lyrical and affirmational poetry with colorful, joyful art. It's a love song to the Spirit, to creativity, and to living life to its fullest." — Carl McColman, author of *Eternal Heart* and *Unteachable Lessons*

"Through intense days, Ally's images help us hold our grief. And in days of ease, their color and vibrancy amplify our joy. In image and word, Ally provides us a luscious feast and true soul kindling." — Alexander John Shaia, author and teacher, www.quadratos.org

"Nourishment lives in these pages. Ally's call to us is both a call to prayer within the fullness of self and a dare to become more and more free in our relationship with Self and the life of the Divine. This book is a bloom on the branch of the tree of life." — Shiloh Sophia, artist, teacher, co-founder and curator of Musea: Center for Intentional Creativity® and Consciousness

"The verses and illustrations on these pages are the work of a gifted poet and artist. 'Love is wide,' says Markotich, asking us to offer 'the very essence of ourselves to a hurting world.' By adding the emotion of her own journey 'to the end of a paintbrush or pencil,' she teaches us how to do the same. Her invitation for the reader to ask themselves what they can do with all that has come to them is not only powerful, but important." — Paula D'Arcy, author of *Waking Up To This Day* and *Stars at Night*

For Josh & Luke

May you always live connected to your wise heart.

I love you.

Contents

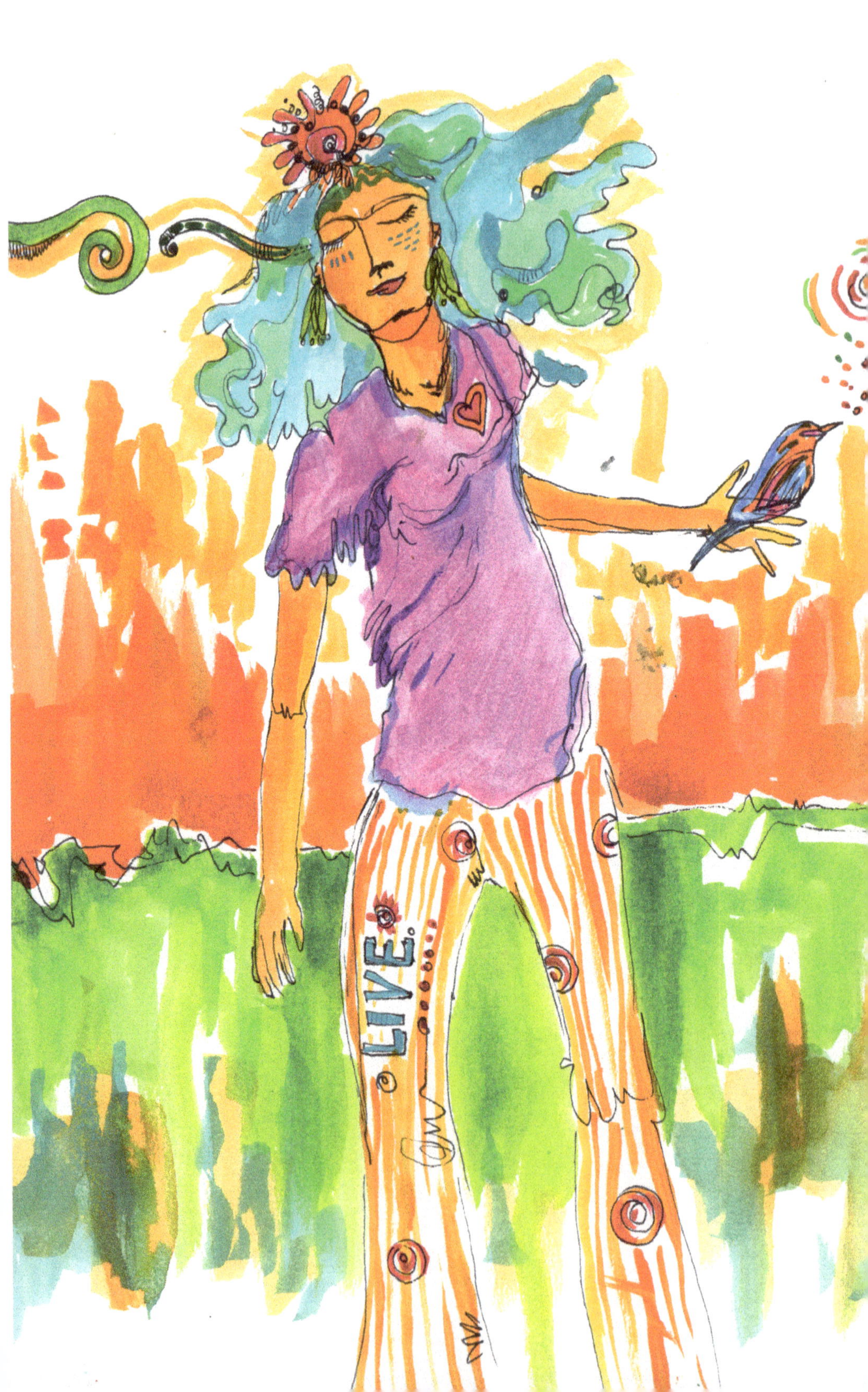
LIVE

Introduction:
The Call that Awaits You

Hello wise one! —
It is clear that you're here
to seek the good news.
The gate is open, the welcome is wide.
Come, color at the table of presence.
Hear the message of love for you.
Loosen your self-imposed limits
and let your sacred imagination lead.
Listen to MotherGod's glad tidings:
You are a creator.
You have a technicolor soul.
Are you ready to (re)member?

WELCOME COLORFUL SOUL

Quiet calls to you. It persuades you to sit. To BE. It invites you to slow down your pace and become present to the grass under your feet. This hush provokes you to notice the beat of your heart. To experience your wise, warm breath within. When you abide, you may sense unnameable enchantment — an alchemy of wind, water, dust and flame — within your very body. This magic may even lead you to hear a tap deep in your soul. A persistent rumble that refuses to stop, interrupting you in the middle of your day and waking you, sometimes, in the obscurity of night. You attempt to brush it aside as nothing, and yet the beat remains.

Little by little, you recognize this nudge as a familiar reminder, a summons to remember. You become aware that this remembrance is not about recent "doings" – like a chore you need to tend to, the dinner you enjoyed last Saturday, or even the vacation you took recently. Rather, it plunges further than that. You catch it as a flash at the edge of your sight. In the waft of baking bread. This inkling tickles your senses to awaken an innate truth you've held since before you were in your mother's womb — and yet, you may have forgotten that it was yours to begin with. You could even be a little scared of the whisper. What might it mean to let go of your resistance? Are you curious to crack the door open and peek at the full-spectrum brilliance that awaits?

I invite you to open your heart to this call. Come, let me take your hand and guide you toward goodness. After all, this recollection is not about something you've been avoiding. It's more like a treasure you've been separated from. A windfall revealing the inner precious jewel of you that has taken to hiding in the daily journey of making safe decisions, attending to others' needs and pressures to please. This is about evoking the still, small voice within – perhaps for the first time – who is always there, calling you home to your true self. Claiming you as a revered gift in this world, loved by the One who knows you and names you as… creator. Inviting you to embrace beauty—yours, and the gift all around you. Not only once, when you were born, but today, tomorrow and, well, every day. Are you beginning to remember? It's about you in the truth of your being – and becoming. Are you starting to recall?

HEALING YOUR SACRED STORY

You may have forgotten, but there is no denying it: You are sacred. You are beloved. You are creative. These are simple enough claims, all of them valid, yet I've discovered that many of us — myself included — have lost our way from these core truths. We've neglected our sacred identity. We've ignored our flicker of radiance and forgotten that we are the salt of the earth. We've cut the cord to the artful

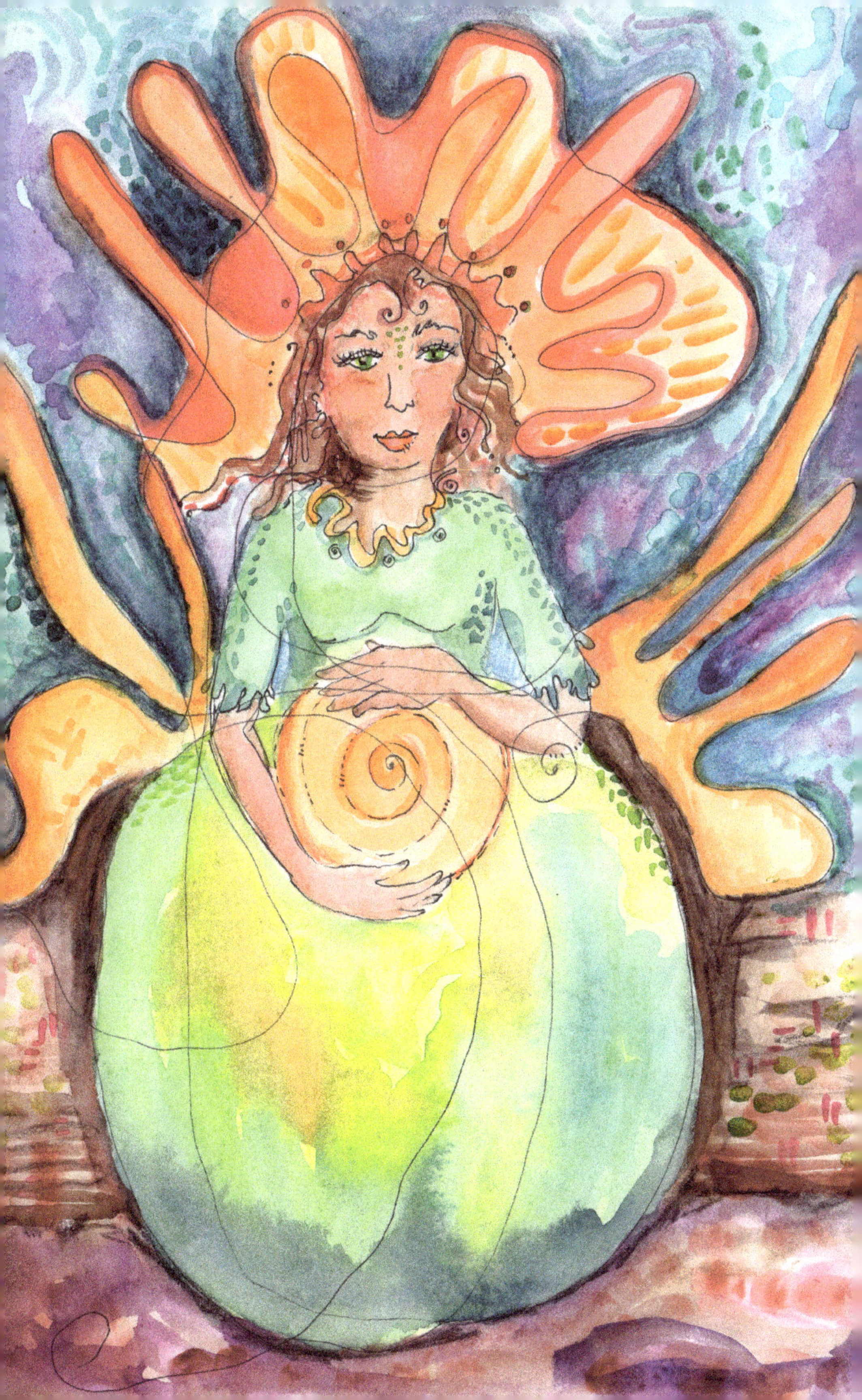

pulse of our be-ing. Which is to say, be-coming. In creating you, MotherGod chose to breathe passion and affection into the immensity of our world through you, speaking the "particular" into form. She celebrates the spark of you. And hails you as a singular gift embraced as a cherished part of this world. Right outside your doors are tall trees of grandeur, clouds drifting by, birds chirping their "hello," water held by the bowl of loving earth — all within the realm of an immense universe — presented as gift, and all of it (including you) named "good." Is this ringing a bell in the hive of your heart? Do you realize that you, too, are woven as a needed thread into the weave of the universe? That you belong to this vital creation, you who are made in the image of Divine Creator?

Do you hear this love rallying you in the recesses of your mind? In those wounded places where you guarded yourself and sought out safety? The Loving One receives you right where you are — and just as you are. Do you recall the color in the marrow of your bones that longs to be expressed? Can you dare to imagine yourself as one with needed wisdom who holds brave ideas?

- Maybe you're already on board to unbind your colors and step wildly into expansion.

- Or, maybe you'd like to believe this is true, but aren't quite there yet.

- Or, maybe you are saying, *No! Not me! I'm not creative. And, this holy love-thing is way out of my comfort zone.*

Listen. It's okay if you've lost touch with the inventive verve that has forever been there, waiting within you. Wondering when you'll come home to who you are in your original self. From the resistances I've faced as well as witnessed in others, I know that this doubt is all too common. Perhaps you are struggling under the burden of harsh wounds that shut the door to your splashy, colorful vivacity – like many in our culture. Plenty among us have hurts we carry from harm done to us – by others, by institutions, and by toxic systems of repression. Perhaps you're one of them. You may have even come to accept false stories that have been told to you. And, what's strange is that you & I tend to hang onto these negative narratives that hijack our artistic be(com)ing and drag them along with us.

Do any of these narratives ring a bell? You've been told you aren't creative and have come to accept it. You diminish yourself alongside others who are deemed "talented" and admit that you're not as good as they are. You convince yourself that your voice isn't made for singing, your feet aren't made to dance. You consider creative work as a lesser pursuit than other "essential" work and so have clipped your wings from trying. You compare your creations with those around you and fall into a competitive trap. You've been labeled "practical" and "logical" which has separated you from your inherent hue so you succumb to a muted existence.

You strain and focus on "getting it right" rather than pausing to name your honest hunger. You've been taught a certain method to pray, yet rote words don't inspire you and you've lost connection with Indwelling Presence. You believe creativity is a luxury that you can't find time for. The unusual thing is your heart realizes these stories are holding you back, yet it takes incredible courage to reject their lure. First, a seed of grace and compassion must be planted, for yourself, and then for others — even for those who've attempted to keep you from discovering and exploring your creative life.

I have good news for you: it's time. Time to plant this seed of grace. Time to draw and paint, to trim and sew a revived story of ingenuity. For yourself, but not only for yourself: for the sake of the world. If I were to imagine creativity as a person, I envision her as a little sassy with a streak of gold in her hair. She is usually up for some good-old-fashioned play, yet she can be hard to pin down. She savors time at the table in intimate conversation, yet when you don't take her seriously, she hides herself. She is certainly rambunctious. Often fierce. Sometimes even rebellious. She is persistent to push boundaries. Some have pressured her to color within the lines. But creativity tends to float, swim and navigate, disregarding those lines to work around walls she comes up against. She also tends to be feared and lusted after (at the same time) by those who don't understand her — she is the mermaid-muse who dives into secret spaces, is sleek and sensuous, and simply cannot be caught. When you abide by her savvy, you become stamped with her mark.

A SUMMONS TO CONNECT

Are you beginning to remember now? You, returning to the Lover of your soul and taking your inherent power seriously, matters. Because you matter. Not the *you* others might have told you about. Or the tamed, voiceless *you* you've reduced yourself to, just to get along from moment to moment. Rather, the genuine *you*. The true *you*. The wild *you* that carries the passion of the mermaid-muse in your innermost essence. This is the source of your be(com)ing. Do you remember her? Him? Them?

When you link to your flavorful zest, you become the artist of your own life. From the clothes you wear to the food you eat, from the words you speak to the actions you take: all of who you are becomes a canvas for the unfolding chroma of your beautiful story. For your becoming… you. No longer does the yarn, *I'm not creative,* guide your choices because you are now waving your mythic paint brush and blazing your path forward.

How do you do this, you might wonder? There is no single lane, no common route. You must find your unique entry which begins when you make room to relate

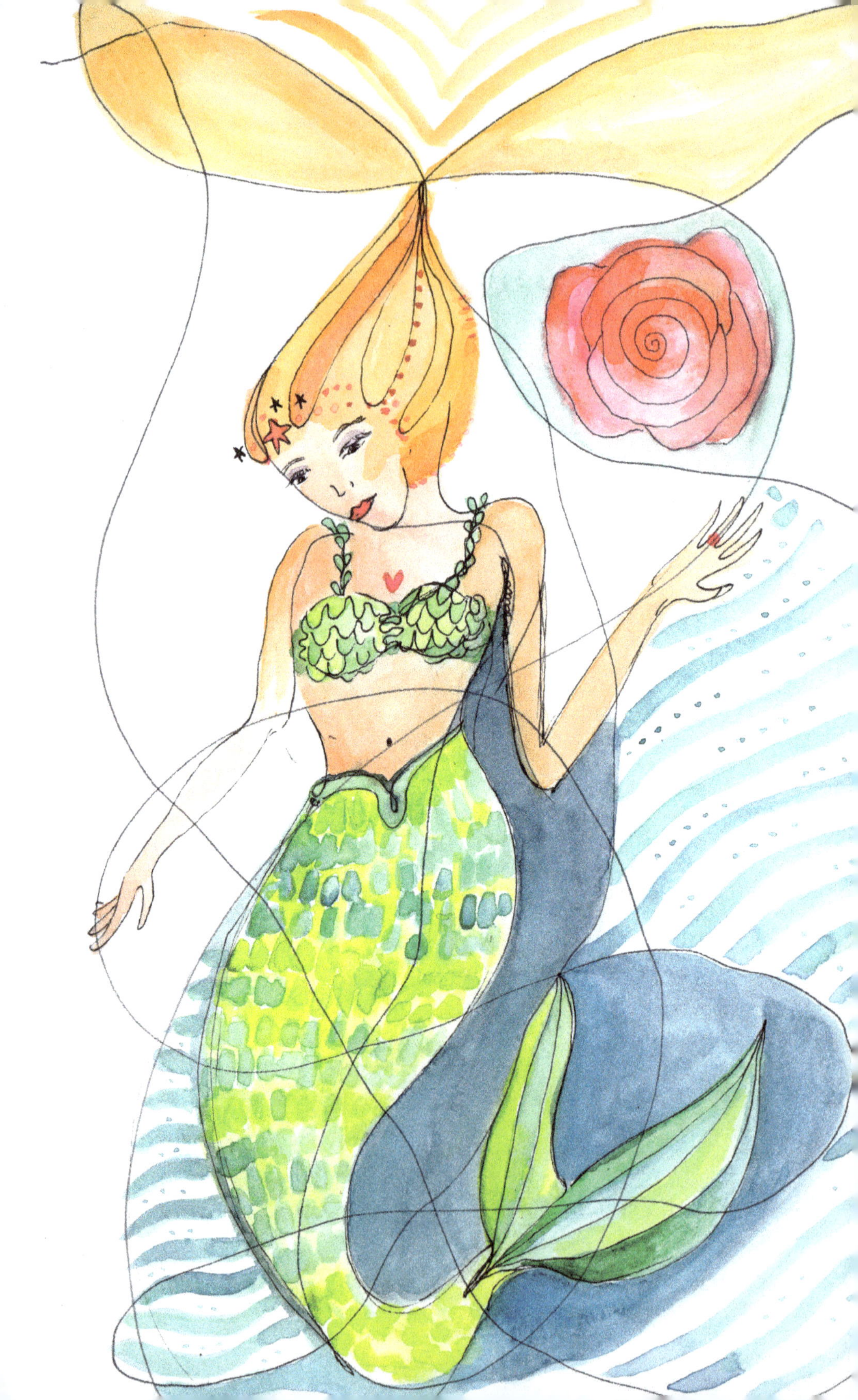

to your inner creator. Regularly. And as you do, you gain more and more access to that sensuous muse within you. Which, in other words, is the source of your essential INsight. That source will guide you to lighten up. To find the courage to dare to begin. To release yourself from the expectation of perfection. To claim the love that is yours – and the beauty that you are! You'll find your ingenuity as you go forward and find yourself able to resist busyness, celebrate beauty and claim your day-to-day course as sanctified — all which enhances the joy you hold. The joy you are.

It may take time to allow your interior judge to ebb. This is the persona that doubts your every mark. *Who are you to create? You're wasting your time. You're going to mess this up.* This voice is often the first one you hear as you open to a blank page or enter into a quiet space. The "judge" loves to protect you at all costs — especially from being vulnerable. And, let's be honest — making a mark on paper reveals a tender side of you. An aspect of you that may be afraid of uncertainty, afraid to release control. This is when your own fierceness is persuaded to prevail. To claim, *I'm here. I'm doing this. No. Matter. What.*

Making room for creative practice is just that — a practice. Distractions will come — your phone will ding, you'll scroll away precious time, a meeting will pop up. You simply must be gentle with yourself and repeat, *Return, return.* When you get away from your practice, return and begin again. Remember that modern day culture trains us to be consumers — we have been wooed to take in other's content — from physical to digital. Many of us have unconsciously layed down our creative powers to consume the work of others. Creative practice is a way to kindle participation with the living Spirit within you — we all have a story that we can actively shape when we enter a space of co-creation.

Creativity is the bridge to your sovereign self. When you take yourself seriously – and say to yourself, *I'm showing up to create no matter what. I'm believing in myself. I'm investing in the materials. I'm setting aside the time and space for this. I'm closing the door to distractions* – something extra-ordinary happens. The holy "inner" you greets the human "outer" you. Your innate wisdom makes her grand appearance. Again. And again. When you enter into partnership with the grace that is "beyond you," this grace reveals her shape within you. Again. And again. The process of creativity becomes a living prayer. You step, perhaps tentatively at first, but with each stride, your confidence rises and your fortitude firms. You sing, perhaps quietly, to yourself, when you begin, but with each note you realize that the world awaits the one song only you can belt.

AN ENCOUNTER WITH THE DIVINE CREATRESS

When you keep to your rhythm of making, another voice emerges. This is the soft whisper of abiding Love that rises — From your heart. From your soul. Who is She? She is MotherGod within — the Creatress of compassion who meets and receives you right here, right now. As you intentionally seek Her and listen to Her good tidings, you come to know She is interested in your wholeness. She is the healing presence who guides you toward forgiveness and release. She cares about your personal expression. She is the sound of favor — where imagination bubbles and brews. She opens the door for whimsy and play to peek their peculiar faces out so you can express joy unabashedly. This hum is the buzz of your inner She-Spirit. She is the giver of fresh visions and a peace beyond understanding to your flourishing heart.

Now, let's be honest. You may be used to referring to the Divine in solely masculine terms. He has been in the spotlight over the ages — as Father; Lord; Shepherd; King. He is the one who connects us with our innate sense of taking action. He encourages a spirit of structure and expansiveness, of outer power and certainty, as you make your way in the world. This is all good. Something of this "get-it-done" notion of the Divine has its place. But this vision leaves much out. Perhaps it has left you out. If you and I only include the masculine when we speak of God, we reduce our experience of the fullness of the Divine. We miss out on the opportunity to heal at a deeper depth within us. We hinder the Sacred Feminine energies of inward reflection, organic flow, and open receptivity that brings balance to the masculine – and an inner integration that brings forth Song. Naming the Divine as "Mother", as "She", is needed in our families, places of worship and wider communities to bring collective healing to our human experience. Giving Her a seat in the sanctuary of our heart opens YOU and I to a blanket of Divine wholeness. Are you ready to learn more about Her?

There's no denying it — the Sacred Feminine is woven intricately into fruitful endeavors. Her threads provide design, sheen, and pattern to the kaleidoscope of you. She is the creative essence, the Spirit that illuminates the hazy spaces of your imaginings. She comes in dreamscapes and leaf-shapes. She embraced you with an everlasting kiss when you came into existence. And, this kiss lingers as you come fuller into your BE-ing. For this kiss blessed and blesses you, in the name of love. And this love has been with you all along. Do you remember Her?

She is Divine — Ma. Matron. Mama. Crone. Wisdom. Eve. Ruah. Mary. Sophia. She is Source. Breath. Creatress. Origin. Gaia. She weaves as a loving parent with Christ and Spirit. She goes by many names and comes from many lands. She is the Eternal One who has been covered up and snuffed out. Her presence has been diminished for thousands of years. And, here She is — requesting you to (re)member — to gather up Her story once again and blend it with your own. Her story is one of relationship, rhythm and rest. She welcomes you to patiently observe the

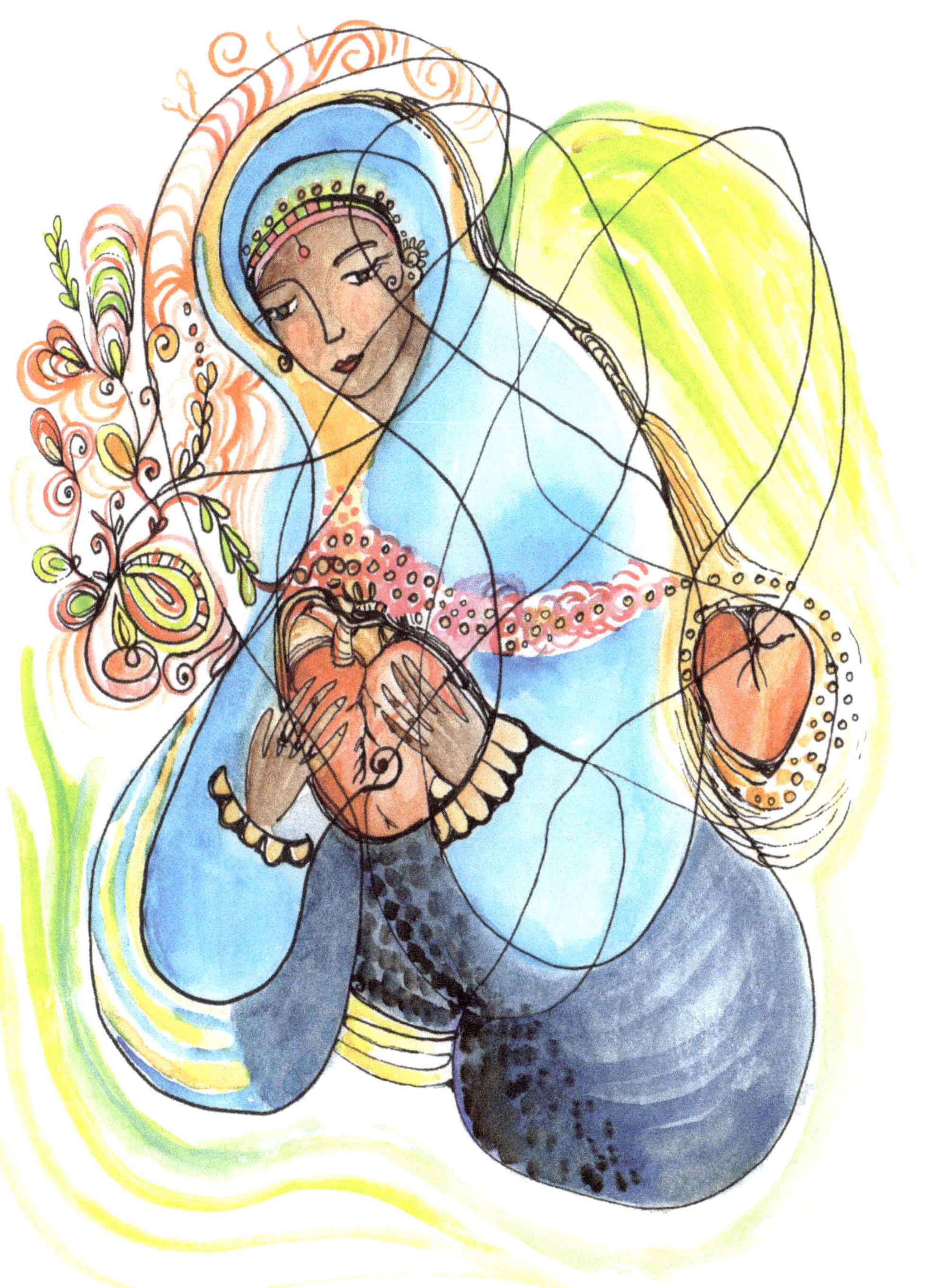

brilliance of your whole body. When you make time to create with intention, you enter into the realm of maternal sensitivity — a cadence of friendship and respite that leads to restoration.

As you create, naturally, you decelerate. Your breathing changes pace. Your lungs open. Yes — it does take bravery to encounter the blank page and imagine into white space. Observation becomes paramount. To witness your marks, words and movements with compassion, not judgment, is important. You'll notice the world you live in with greater detail — the people you encounter, the land you live on, the animals you spy. Drama falls to the background as original inquiries peak — *How do I create seafoam blue? What shape is the eye? Who would I become if I expressed from my heart?* You may even become more aware of the many rhythms that govern nature — the moon, the day, the seasons, the body — all of which include an expansion into fullness and a waning into rest and recovery. Haste falls to the wayside. Surface friendships don't survive — because the depth of Mother Wisdom leads you to knead Her darkness — and here you encounter a nourishment that soothes your vast wholeness and urges you to pursue others who have entered Her realm.

One of the beautiful secrets of the Sacred Feminine is that She is not interested in production. She is unconcerned about a perfect piece of art or a creation that you can sell to the masses. Rather, She invites you to be in relationship to the beauty you are making. Energize your loving intention into now. Release your red-hot pain. Beat a rhythm of fragmented frustration. Mix up a concoction of raspberry cheer. Paint pleasure. Draw a pattern of natural elements. When you come to create, you are invoked to name why you are there — to claim the story that is yours and release the pressure of what you "should" make. The more you enter this friendship, the more you'll distinguish the marks, colors and style that belong to you. You'll encounter your tone of articulation. This is cause for celebration! You have arrived to yourself and the world in which you live and your unique devotion reverberates out.

Your time and devotion to the Mother heals the wounds of her forgotten nature within you. Inevitably, you'll hear Her care rise as you continuously show up to create. As you chant, spin and drum, there She is with you. As you cook delicious food, there She is with you. As you draw, paint and color, there She is with you. As you wake early to write, there She is with you. As you throw and glaze your clay pot, there She is with you. As you plant wildflower seeds in your garden, there She is with you. As you lie down to rest, there She is with you. As you study and learn, there She is with you. As you speak the words only you can speak, and listen to the silences only you can hear, there She is with you. Her presence will not be wiped clean by human attempts, because She has been here since the beginning. And, here is the good news — Her embrace is wide open as you explore the art and musings in this book. Which is to say, as you discover yourself becoming who are you.

AN INVITATION TO BEGIN

This book holds rich art and poetic inspirations for you to remember yourself as a creator, cherished by the Eternal Flame. It's a companion for you to visit often so the lamp of your heart remains lit. There are many means to create and the kinetic words here are meant to ignite you to move through your fear and set off with a small practice that suits you. My deep wish is that as you read, gaze and ignite your creative spark, you will set out to share the spectrum of who you are, authentically, in the world. Together, when we commit to tending our personal genius, we bring healing and care into the spaces we roam and the relationships we hold.

Four sections of thirteen poems each are included to accompany you on your life path, across the arc of a year or through your whole life:

Root: I Am Creative — If you've ever lost your way from the spark of yourself or have wondered, *Who Am I?*, then pause in this section to read poetry and view art related to identity. Rediscover yourself as a sacred, creative being.

Breathe: I Am Pilgrim — When you leave what you've known to set out towards new territory, the road can be full of challenges and questions even as the sun peaks her face. Stop in this section if you are moving through a transition and need a reminder that you don't go alone on your journey.

Spark: I Am Wonder — Everyone needs a little zest in their lives! This section is full to the brim of poems and art to peek your imagination and awaken you to the buzz of life that is within and all around.

Flow: I Am She — The Sacred Feminine is here! The poems found in this section reconnect you with the gift of anima energy found in all beings. Whether you are new to the idea of the Sacred Feminine or have been in relationship with Her for some time, you are invited to pause here to stretch your notion of who She is and where She is on your daily travels.

WAYS TO ENGAGE THIS BOOK

There is no "one right way" to immerse yourself into this book. This is not a book of one-two-three steps. It is not a linear story. Thus, there is no reason to read this book from first page to last. Give yourself permission to ruminate leisurely with the poems and art. Allow them to be a catalyst to rouse the creative nature that lives within you. You will notice there is a repetition of themes and words; this is intentional. I have found that I must hear a message many times, said in different ways for it to root in my heart — maybe this is true for you, too. As you read, ask yourself *What desires to be birthed through me?* You may be surprised at what your heart speaks — an old camera may want to be dusted off; a rhythm on the radio may lead you to dance with fervor; a party you've hoped to plan may finally come to fruition. And, if you are hesitant to dip your toes into these sacred, creative waters, become curious about your resistance. As you take in the words and visuals, receive them as seeds being planted within you. Who knows what beauty will grow if you open yourself to the possibility that you are indeed a creative, holy human who belongs wholeheartedly wherever you roam.

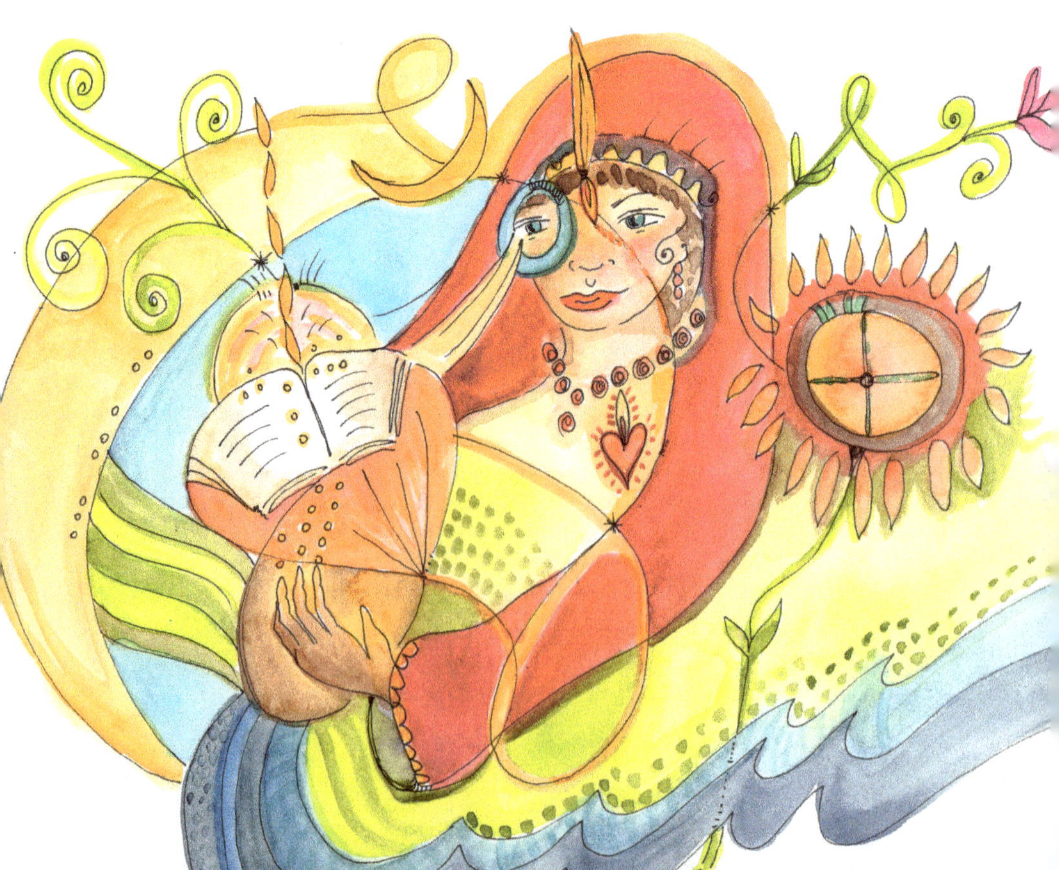

Contemplative Ways to Curate Your Creative, Sacred Spark

- ***Loosen Your Grip.*** Close your eyes, open to a random page and let your finger roam on the page and point. Open your eyes and take the word or (portion of) the image and let your pen doodle and draw with this concept at heart. Engage a sense of whimsy and playfulness.

- ***Slow Down and Listen.*** Linger with one poem each week. Choose the poem that calls to you and revisit it throughout the week. Let it simmer within you as you navigate your days. If you feel led, you can keep a journal and write about your gleanings. Consider the practice of *Lectio Divina* to guide you. *Lectio Divina* is a way of reading for *formation* rather than information. You are not reading to learn facts or get to the end. Rather, you are slowing down to read and meet with the living Spirit. By focusing on the same reading repeatedly, and returning to it often, you might find that a personal prayer, message or invitation to transformation will come to you in unexpected moments and ways. Open yourself to surprise. A common approach to *Lectio Divina* is as follows:

  » First, choose a poem and read it (or a portion of it) aloud, if possible.

  » Then, read it again and see what word or phrase shimmers.

  » Listen or read a third time and reflect on the invitation of this word or phrase in your life; allow your curiosity to lead you in directions you could not anticipate.

  » Read a fourth time and rest.

- ***Focus and Ignite.*** Commit two weeks to reading one poem per day from the section that draws you in. Complete each day's reading by responding to the theme with your personal, creative expression — Draw. Paint. Journal. Walk. Chant. Dance. Sing. Spin. Weave. Be you.

- ***Gaze and Be.*** Choose an image that calls to your heart. In the way that Lectio Divina is a practice of slow, meditative reading of the Bible (or some other meaningful text), I'm inviting you to practice the art of *Visio Divina*. Visio Divina is a deliberate way to gaze and ponder, linger, and reflect. By spending time with an image, details become clearer to us than on a first glance; we might even find that messages from Spirit arise. Similar to *Lectio Divina, Visio Divina* is a practice of (trans)formation. Rather than taking in an image for consumption, you are invited to participate with it.

To hear what it may reveal to you for your life. A common practice of *Visio Divina* is as follows:

» Scan over the entire image slowly. Take in the entirety.

» Now, scan the image again. What area of the image calls to you?
  Focus on this detail of the image with curiosity for a minimum of thirty seconds.

» Continue to gaze. Linger as you listen. Do you hear a prayer or invitation rising for you based on the detail?

» Complete by returning your gaze to the entirety of the image. When you are ready, write or doodle about the invitation/prayer in your journal.

YOUR TIME TO SHINE

The time has come for you to re-member yourself as the sacred, creative being you are. The essence of YOU cannot be taken away. As you set forth, I encourage you to be gentle with yourself. Listen carefully to what you need. Let yourself nap. Take a bath. Go outside and get lost in nature. Release your grip a little and let uncertainty lead. Once you've filled up with sacred breath and rest, *then* open to a blank page and unfurl a line, unleash your words, make your movement. Allow the words and images in this book to guide your creative adventure. Be slow in reading, returning and notice the way the themes begin to simmer within you. Remember, there is no "right" way to create. You, blessed one, are the holder of your own expression. Part of the journey is learning to trust the Wisdom you were given before you were born and allow it to be birthed through you. This means you must try and try again. And again.

I urge you to keep showing up to the work of your own creation. Add your love and intention into what you make. Let the process of creating become your prayer. Pay attention to the materials you enjoy working with and the materials you don't. Notice if you enjoy making fast marks or slow; open yourself to luxurious washes of color. What patterns and symbols want to make their way from your hand? Observe your words, images and creations with curiosity, not judgment. Ask questions of yourself. As you relink to yourself as a sacred, creative being, you'll find that relationship with the Source of Love in myriad facets — nature, animals, metaphors, symbols, textures, and on and on — naturally deepens. Become interested in the world within yourself and the world around you and

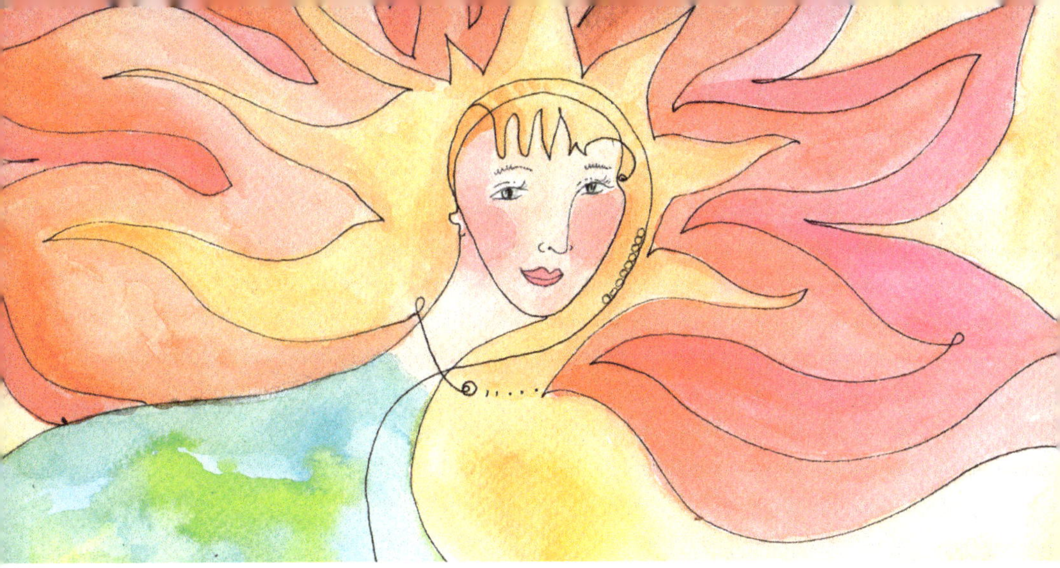

you'll find your way back to your colorful, divine spark over time. I am cheering you on in your creative pursuit and celebrate the imprint of you in this holy, human place we call home. I am with you.

With all my love,

P.S. There is a bite-sized creative prayer practice called, ***Prayer Squares***, at the back of the book to gently guide you into your colorful expression. Prayer Squares is a simple, 4-step spiritual practice for all ages to spark prayer life in a fun and fresh way! With a pencil, black permanent marker and color of your choice, Prayer Squares invites you to pour out, listen in and allow your inner Divine love to arise through word, line, color and reflection. This is my regular go-to practice. What I love most about it is the surprising revelation that this invites in only ten to fifteen minutes of creative time.

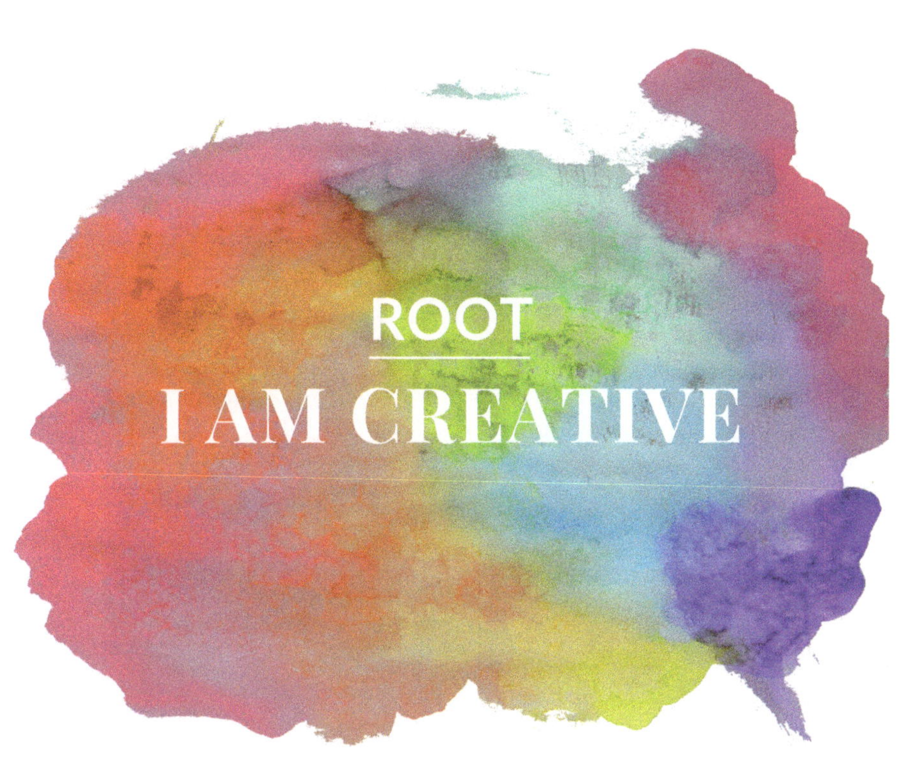

Re-member Your Sacred,
Colorful Foundation

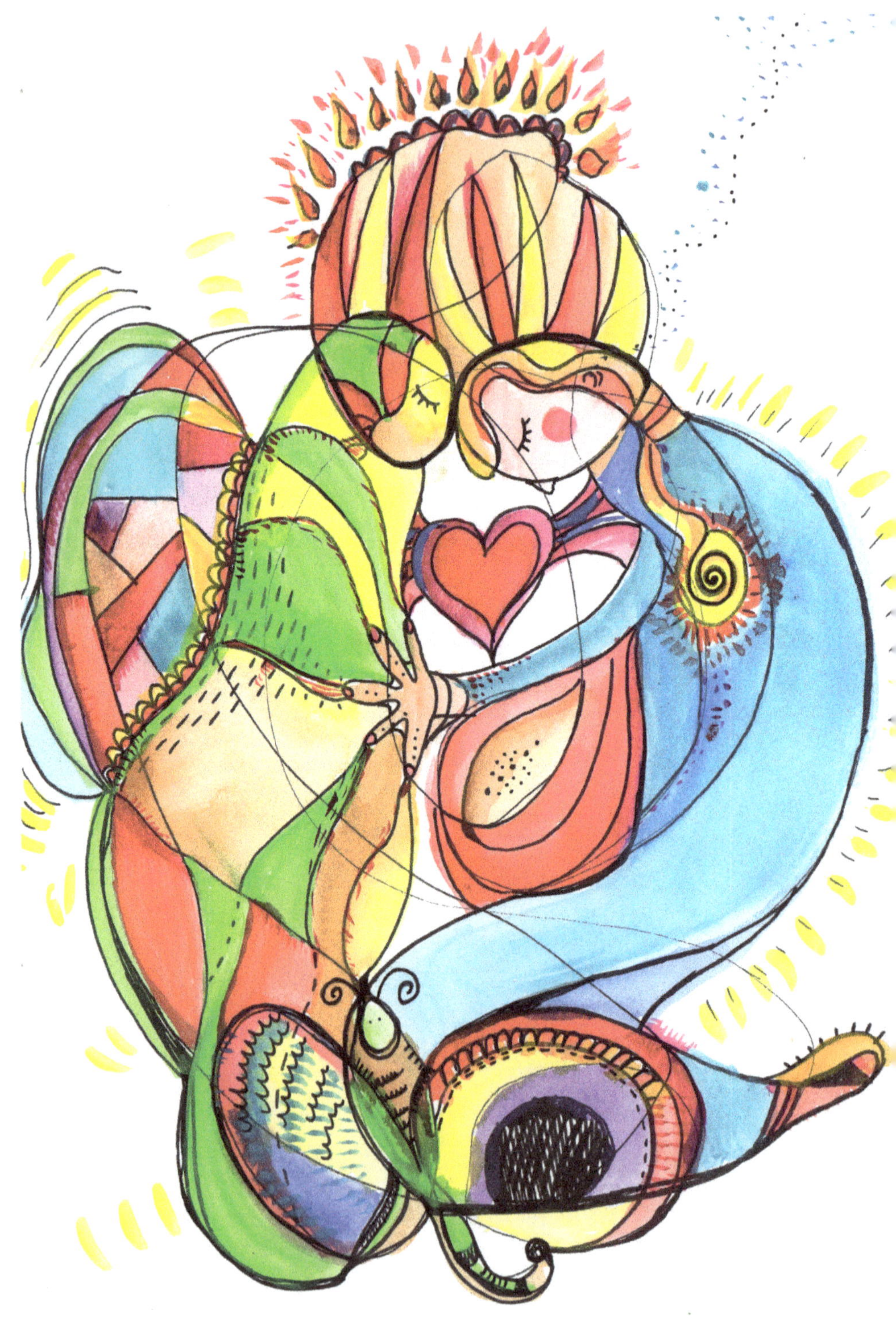

WHAT DOES IT TAKE TO BE AN ARTIST?

I sit on the stone steps at twilight
and look at the emerging moon.
I speak aloud the question
I've been carrying for some time:
What does it take to be an artist?

Does it take paintings in galleries
with big, fancy openings?
Is it a book announcing my name on
a shimmery spine placed in a bookshelf?
Does it take the right amount of schooling
with perfect technique and advanced degree?

Of course,
what I'm really asking is,
Am I an artist?

I realize that children never court this query.
They dare to have faith in themselves
as the amazing artists they are – and it is so.

This night, I make a bold decision.
I change my direction.
Instead of saying goodnight to the moon,
heading to bed wistful at heart —

I step into the peculiar darkness and
walk into the wide, wild world.
For the first time, I notice how moonlight
makes the most interesting shadows.

The pitter-patter of love leads,
external voices ebb,
an echo of resonance emerges,
one I remember from long ago:
my own.

My inherent words float,
Practice creative work. Simply practice.

Aha! Clarity. Practice is key.
How had I forgotten?

I fold my hands in prayer,
bow to myself, the moon, and the Great Beyond.

I understand what I must do.
I commit to showing up for myself.

My instinct guides me.

As I press, I put my fingers
on the pulse of creation.
I devote myself to the unknown.
My giddy heart anticipates
what will appear on the blank page.

I don't understand the why or how.

This doesn't matter.
I trust the magnetic pull
of unexplainable force.

I raise my hands in gratitude
to streaming Spirit, sailing Christ,
and speak with quiet resolve:

Thank you for this egg of an idea.
I will nurture it to completion
and watch it fly into the sunset.

Now I grasp that "artist"
has everything to do
with the risk
of making my brave swath
in the world –
with the mark of
me.

As an artist
you give the very essence
of yourself as an offering
to a hurting world

and place your
rainbow band-aid on
one aspect of
the tear.

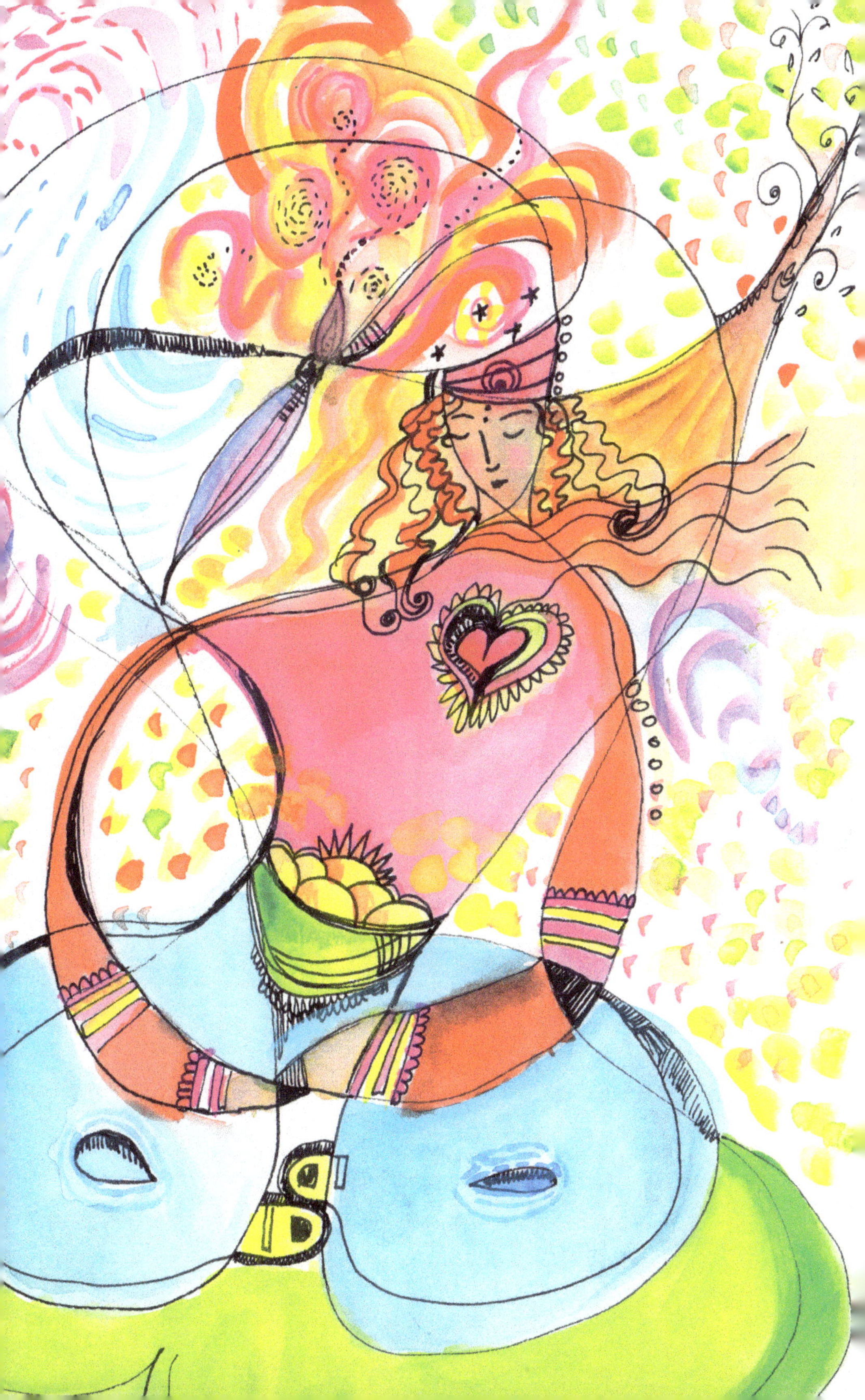

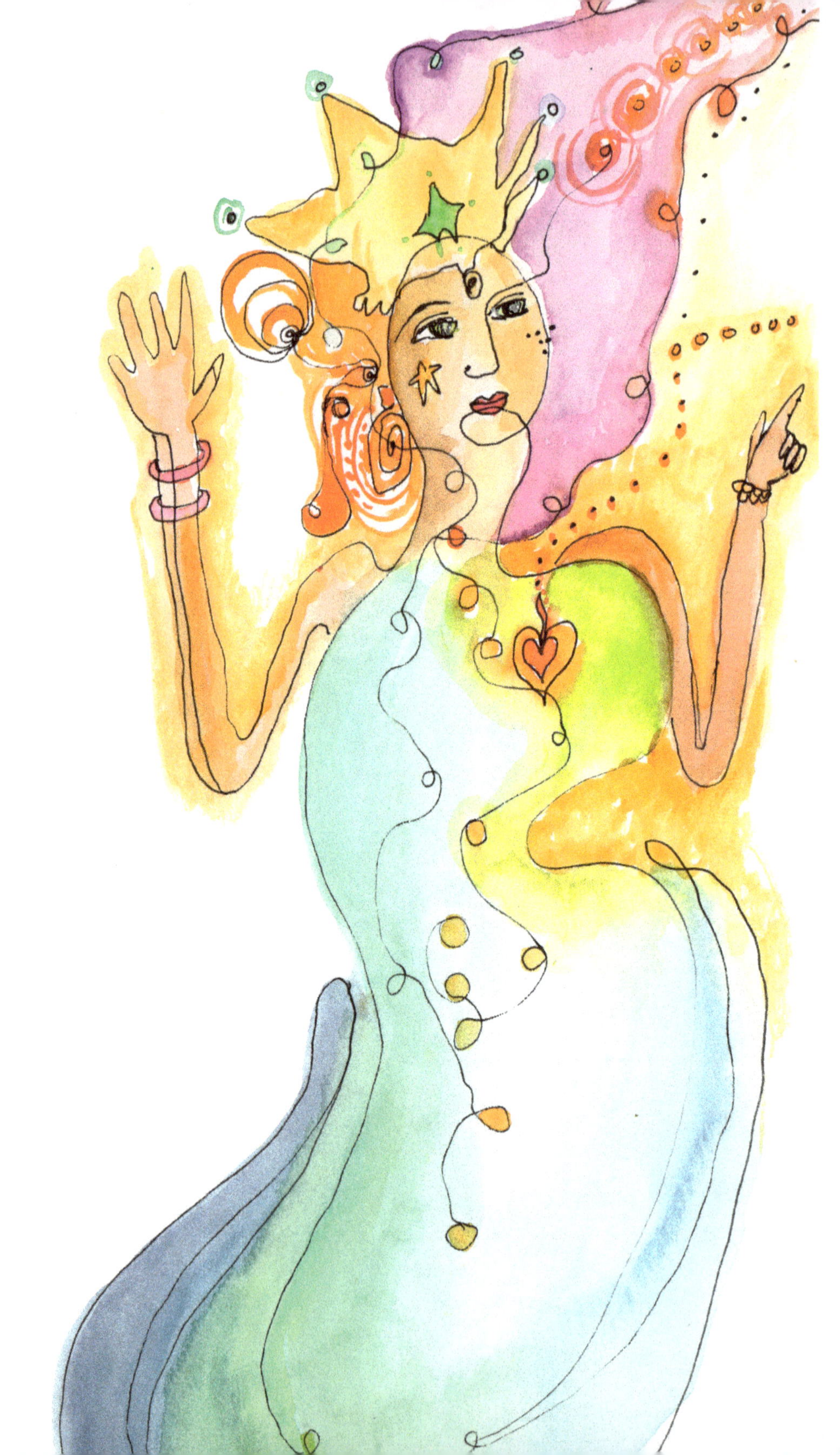

These days,
you'll find me saying,
Yes, I'm an artist!

I believe you are too.

Be brave.
Make your mark.
Today.
Now.

WEARER OF THE CROWN

Hey.
Pssst.
You.
Wearer of the crown—
     Who, ME?
Yes, you.
     No, no, no.
     You must be mistaken.
     I don't wear a crown.
Sure, you do.
I see it.
     Are you looking at me?
(laughs) Yup, yup. Sure am.
Your crown is beautiful.
Very intricate.
     Well
     (pause)
     What does it look like?
Oh, honey.
Sure is splendid. Looks like
hundreds of owl feathers waving high,
pearls from the depths of the ocean
placed with precision,
flecks of gilt woven with mighty care.
And, oh my!
I spot a unicorn hair.
     Why can't I perceive my crown?
Remember that wonderful story
The Polar Express?
And the message that believers
must have ears to hear?

Well, sweetheart,
your divinity was assigned
to you as you were knit
in your mama's womb.
Your holy twinkle
is sure as the ocean tide;
there's *nothing* you can do
to take it away,
and no one
can take it from you.
OH!
when you
open...open
to MotherGod's reception of you;
when you
open...open
to the notion that
you, indeed, sport a crown—

well,
then, you begin
to behold,
to really behold,
pure, delectable
treasures like
tiaras made
with fallen oak leaves,
plump burgundy berries,
washed up shell of abalone
sparkling upon
the heads
of all.

You begin to know
— to really know —
all people as
royal daughters,
royal sons,
all wearers of crowns
who are
children of
creative Love.
>*You're telling me that if I begin to trust that I wear a crown;*
>*I'll actually witness it myself? That I'll discover my own crown?*
Indeed.
>*Me? Royal? And others, too? All wildly sacred?*
More than you can fathom.

Whether you notice a crown or not
makes no difference,
you remain
adored by MotherGod who Loves.
>   *What you're suggesting feels preposterous!*
>   *If not absurd!*
>   *I mean, I really need to stretch my comfort zone*
>   *to believe I wear a crown!*
>   *AND*
>   *even more so to think*
>   *those different from me wear one!*
Yes, and when you take the leap to trust,
you'll be changed forever. For then
the gates of heaven will be open to you
here on earth.
>   *Me? A crown wearer? Already here and now?*
>   *Hmmm…*

BURST INTO YOU

There is
nothing
I crave more
than for you
to burst into

yourself — to become
who you are.

I hear you talk
of one thing,

yet detect
your hidden world
of bells and whistles
humming inside —

where your
dreams live and
visions churn.

Has the sound of the bell subdued?
The shimmer of the whistle lost its luster?

Well, then,
maybe you need a
summertime sabbath—

time to dip your hands into ocean water,
crunch your toes on mountain leaves or
nap quietly in a swinging hammock

wherever you need to go to hear

the sound of you again
(the sound of you loving yourself again);
please go there. Now.

Listen—
if I could trek your trail for you,
I would.
But the truth is,
this is a path you must take for yourself,
a choice only you can make.
You can decide to set forth. YOU CAN take action
on behalf of yourself.

Yes, you matter.
Yes, you are loved.
Yes, you deserve the time.

Lay down the belief
that you must make others happy first.

Hooey!

Joy awaits you
when you release your grip
to listen and linger
with the inquiries of your own soul:

Who am I?
What stirs my imagination at midnight?
What is the offering I bring to creation's feast?

Do you hear your still small voice?
What it thirsts for?

Of course there is risk.
This is the free-fall
the Spirit of Courage

emboldens you take.
Please —
unlock your inner door,
the one that's been rattling
since time began.

When you do,
I'll be waiting
on the other side
to celebrate your

star-spangled entrance.

QUEST OF A CURIOUS GIRL

In Memory of Kristen Rietkerk

O curious one,
you, the delightful —
one who doesn't
gulp others' words as your own.
You who slowly sip ideas,
swallow deliberately,
muse over the how,
the wonder,
the *what could be.*

Hello, twinkle toes, you
twirler and tapper of the earth —
banners of blush beam with every bounce you make.
Stardust speckles anticipate your entrance,
succumb to your eager look.
When told to gaze plainly at the galaxy,
you plunge your arms into the haze of black sky
to touch the buzz of lustrous glitter on your fingers.
Your tippy toes help you open yourself to a glorious gleam.
When told not to get near the fire,
you toss kindling toward the heat to smell the smoky air,
watch sparks ignite.
When they do, your insides jump and
join you with energy beyond yourself.
Don't deny it. It's beautiful and true.
You are the one who plunges
into the ocean of your heart,

not looking for answers,
but longing to live with abandon,
to uncover facets of your diamond self,
to swim among rainbow coral
and learn from the murky shadows.
Not satisfied with black and white certainties,
you learn from even the zebra who ponders,
Am I black with white stripes or white with black stripes?
to beg questions after the Divine One's presence —
Is the light here? Or there?
Do I need to spin to the right or hop to the left?
You persevere, not satisfied with others' answers,
but on a search for your own burning blaze,
to discover the source of Divinity within, the One
who leads your approach to life
altered in strange fashion.

When you encounter those who point to the true vine,
you let their words turn to honey sweetening your soul,
And, you BraveSoul,
are the brazen strand who boldly proclaims
Here I am, let it be to me as you have said.

You are the one who considers it joy
wherever the trail of wonder leads.

YOU AND THE STARS

The stars danced the salsa
the night you were formed —
aware they were part of you
and, you, a part of them.

The stars burned bright
when your spark came into being —
when you mattered, simply
because you became matter.

The stars shone upon you
as you toddled your childhood tempo —
glistened their watchful devotion
as your curiosity emerged.

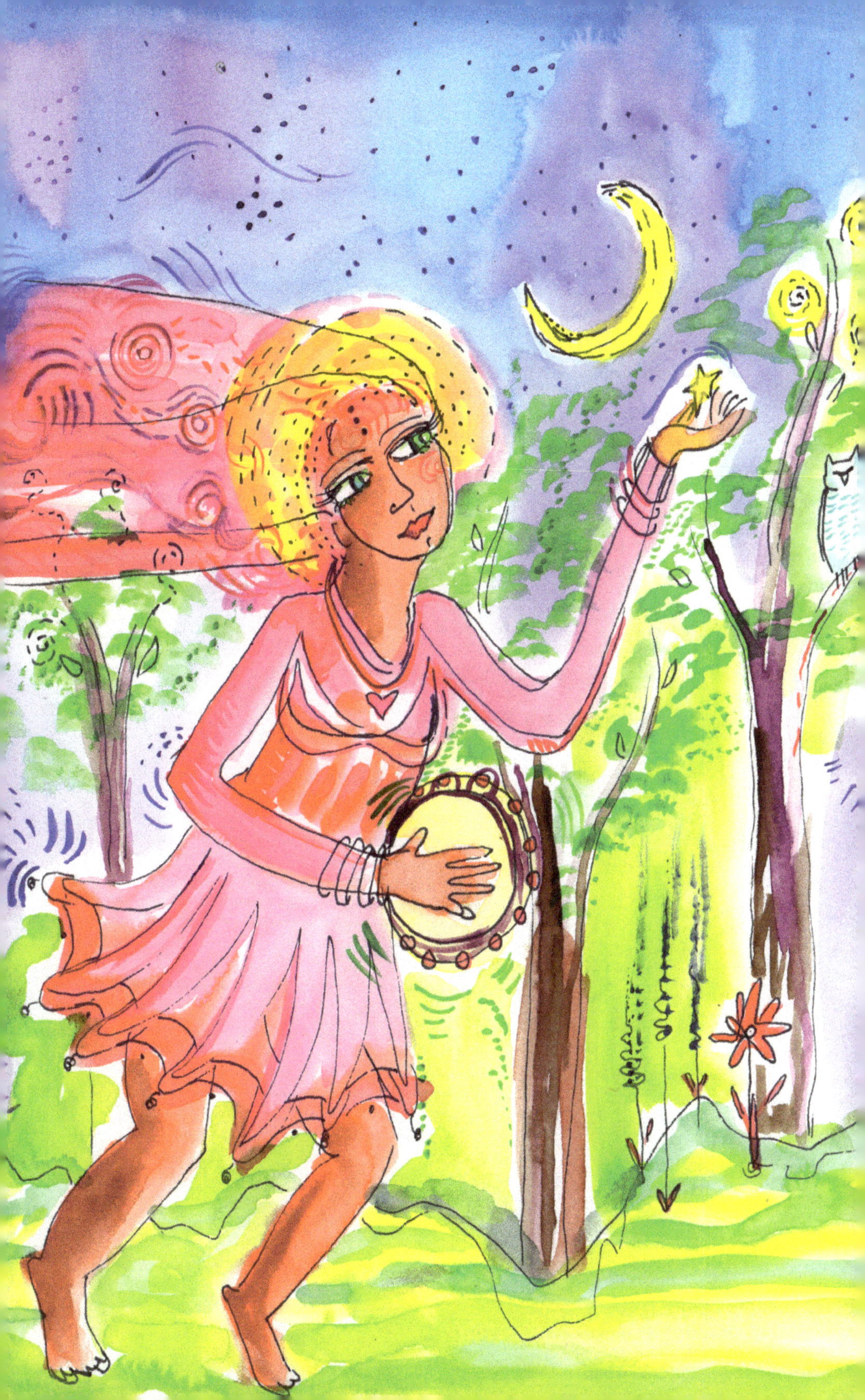

Those orbs of fluorescent juice, billions of years old,
followed your figure while you figured it out —
gave you direction a blink at a time
for your weary traveling bones.

Despite —
gray clouds,
your fleeting glance,
rapid pace of days gone by,
the stars remained —
a far flung umbrella of love.

This very ordinary eve
the stars beam their rays over you,
their constellation of stories sings —
urges you to listen for your own tale
to awaken to your shared link.
You and the stars,
hitched from the beginning —
friends forever, the twinkle
cannot be forsaken.

HANDS OF CREATION

I hold a secret behind the curtain.
This secret is too good to keep to myself.

After all,

secrets need fresh air to breathe
AND they need spoken breath
to transform into something delicious.

I'm ready to tell you.
Are you listening?

Here it is:

EVERYONE has hands of creation.

Now, you may not think this is a big deal.
Or… you may look at your own hands and think,
What… my hands? You must be mistaken.

No. I am NOT kidding you.
THIS is serious whimsy-ness.
I urge you to untie the tales that keep your hands bound —

you know the one — where your hands have nothing important to add.
This, a downcast story – do you sense your shoulders crouch?

Or this one — the belief your hands need to control creation.
This, a dangerous rumble — do you feel your belly quake?

It's time for a stronger faith, a truer conviction:
There, let your hands be a conduit *FOR* creation,
a hollow flute for fortune to flow through,
a communion with the splendor within.

Keep one eye closed to conceive,
one open to hone your attention,

one hand behind the secret veil,
one caressing the pulse of creation.

THIS is the access to where and how ideas abound.
THIS is the clue to what YOUR hands want to form.
THIS is the passage to a thriving life.

The secret has been with you all along:
You, the holder of two ripe hands
ready to grow something beautiful.

All you need to do is —
release your grip.

I AM BECOMING

I

am

becoming.

I'm not finished yet. No,
I still have loads of color to splash around.
A palette of rainbow
to fling toward the universe.

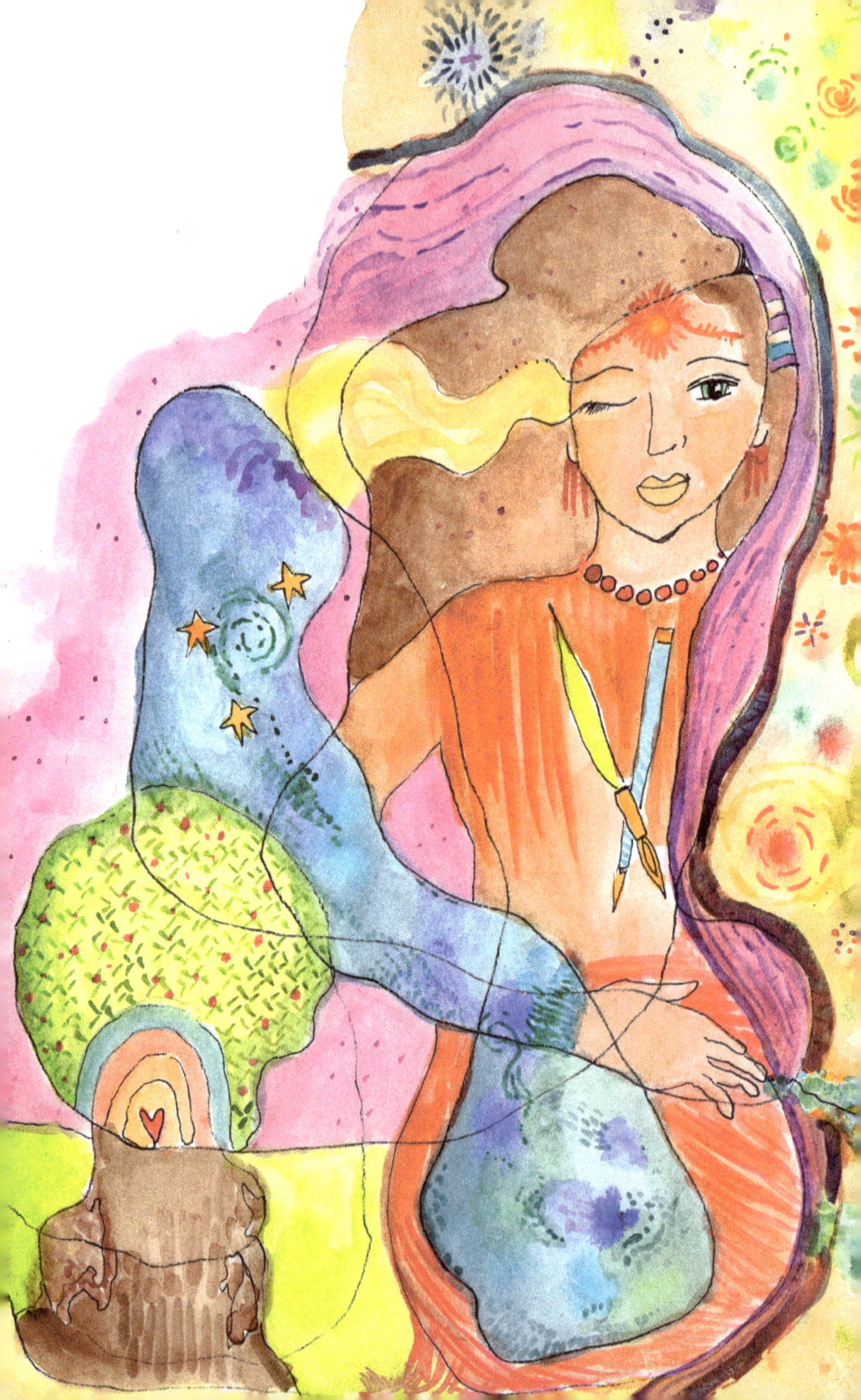

I have unique words to whirl
into the purple galaxy.
A bag of letters and words
to share with those who seek.

You may not see me
much these days —
Don't you know?
Caterpillars need time
to morph into a merry monarch.

I

am

becoming.

I move to the drumbeat of the soul,
sway my hips to the rhythm of Spirit
where it takes me — who can tell?

I don't listen with my brain
but the whole of my being—
heart, gut, mind, tingles in my fingers.

My intention is sharp and shiny as a battle sword.
My loyalty is fierce and gentle as a mama wolf.
My eyes search for beauty in the gaze of another.

I

am

becoming.

I flow to where the genuine grows.
My methods don't make sense to most.
Why would they?
None have spent time in my stride.
They don't understand the blaze in my blood.
The spark that set me off.

I

am

becoming. . .

myself.

Ain't that a glorious sight!

REBORN

Breaking
Emerging
Rebirthing
of oneself —
A painful process

Ugly
Kicking
Screaming
Wriggling
Plunging Under
Breathless Awakening

Is there a sound when a cocoon splits open?

Was resistant
Now broken open
Sputtering
Wobbling
Finding solid ground
Spreading soft wings
Awkward
Gawking
Strange
And
Freedom too
Deep Blessed Freedom

Flapping wings
to Launch
and Fly.
Fearless.

FABRIC OF YOU

Girl,

You be you.
Who else you gonna be?

You've worn —

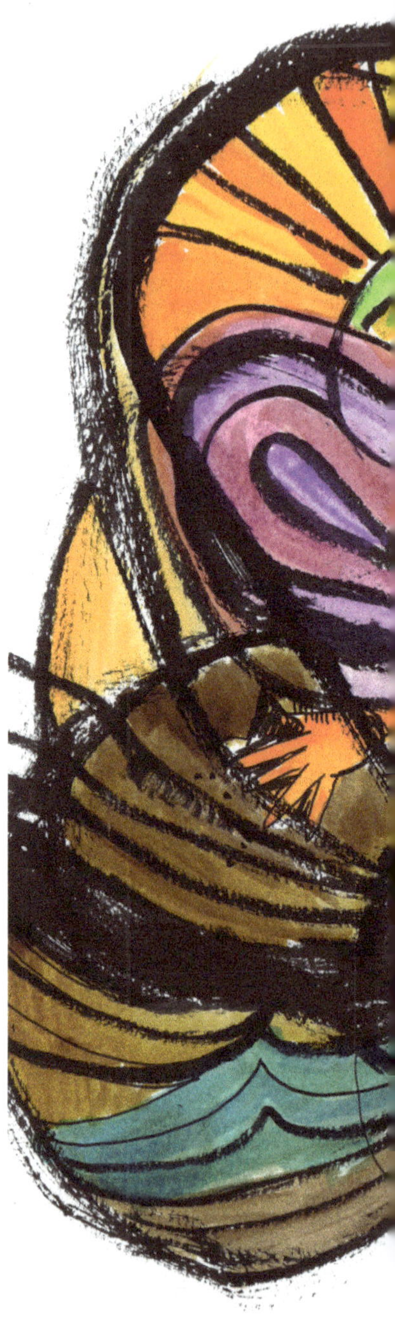

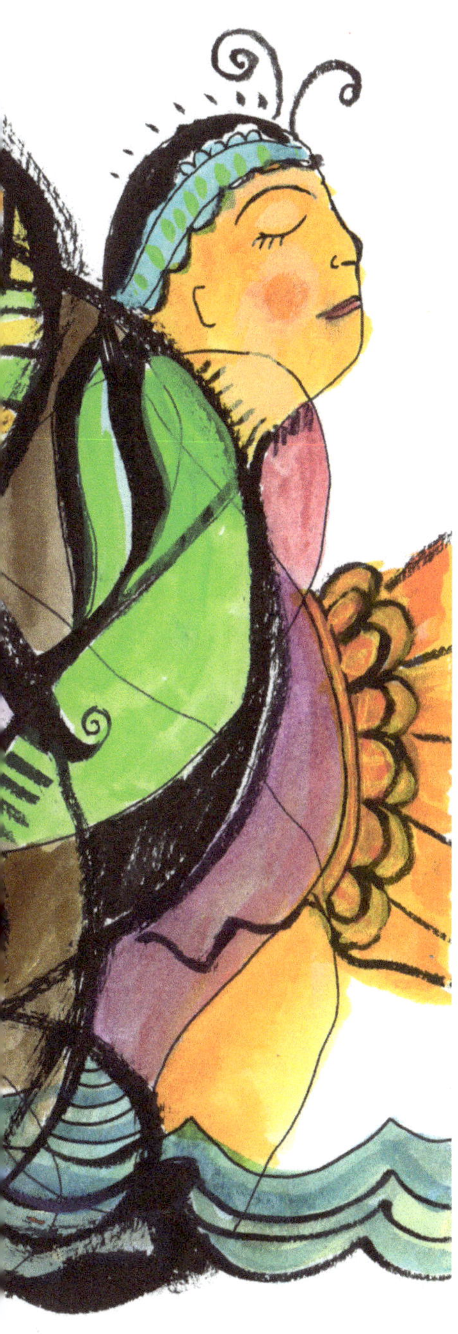

passive smirks,
lit-up eyes,

faded jeans,
clubbin' heels,

opinions of the crowd,
desire from your core,

fit-in chameleon,
unique chic,

pouted lips,
head-back laugh,

insecure thoughts,
Wisdom truth,

peacock proud,
glory to Beyond,

sleek black garb,
chromatic cascade,

narrow critique,
open perspective,

You've clothed yourself with —

either/or,
both/and,

slumped shoulders,
confident promenade,

silent voice,
articulate words,

point & blame,
admit your fault,

wrestling obedience,
servant leadership,

group gatherings,
serene solitude,

FatherGod, here's my offering,
          MotherGod, show me your way,

prove, prove, prove,
          I am enough,

rancid judgment,
          caring compassion,

feel-good gossip,
          encouraging words,

senseless worry,
          bold prayer,

temperamental outburst,
          receive what comes.

You've tried, girl,
one thousand ways
to BE.

Take a swatch
of what you've learned
from each
and BECOME.

Sew it into
the changing fabric of you.
Grateful
for all that is
and isn't.

This is your opportunity
to receive grace
from Alpha and Omega
for the WHOLENESS
of you.

So, celebrate!

You BE you becoming.
Who else are you gonna be?

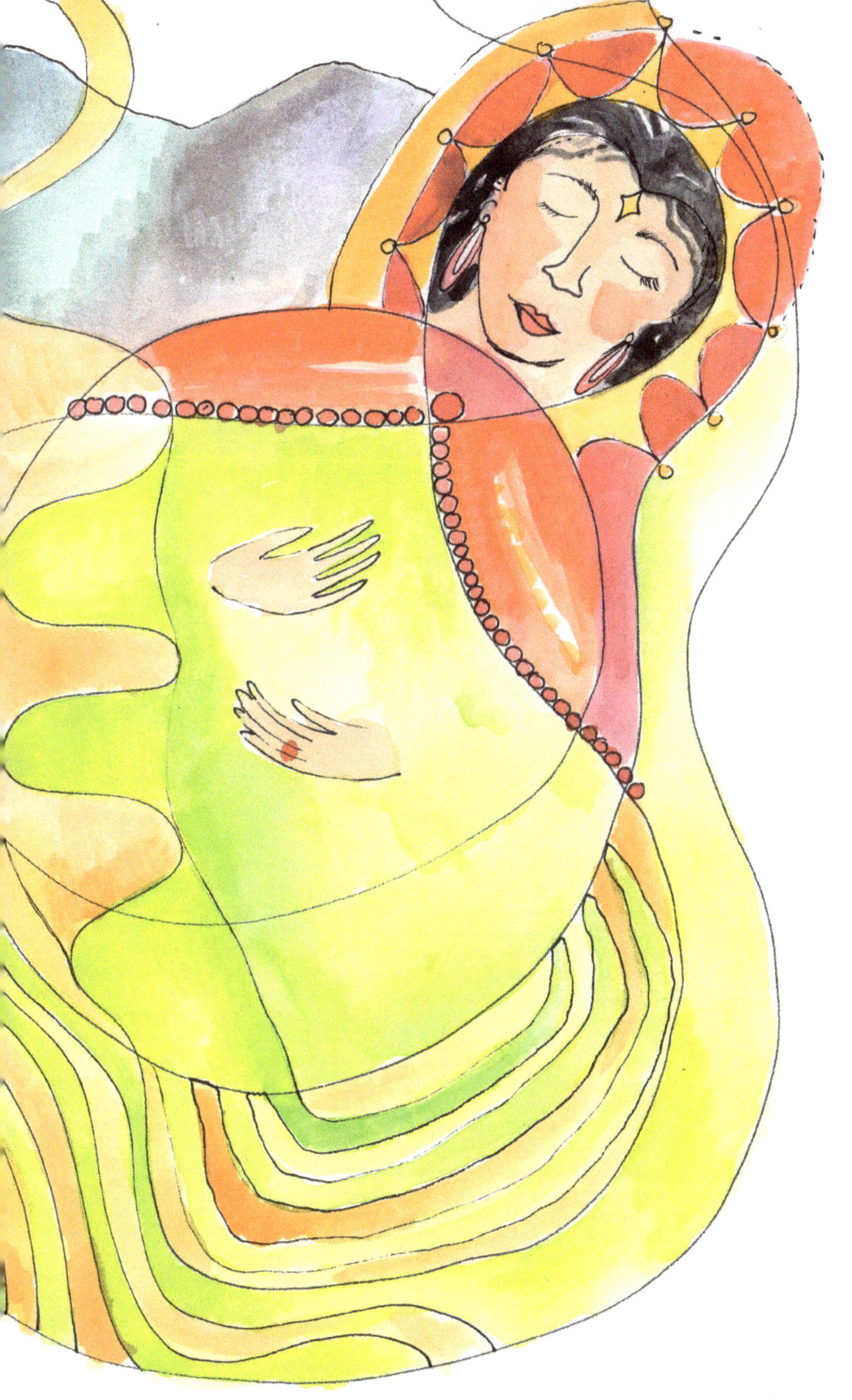

BEAUTIFUL FLAWS

When it all bears heavy,
your fixed flaws,
petty imperfections,
mortal error,
wretched rejection,
irreverent thoughts,
voices from the past,
unholy actions,
your whimpering, weak
human you.

Be still. Stand firm. You are here.
Be present to the pressure at breaking point.
As the cracks in your perfect veneer emerge,
     (simply pause)
take an ample breath.
     (pause again)
Look at your sheen stream through each rift.

Dear one,
you need the cracks.
Your flaws are your beauty.

Do you hear the cry
in the garden of your spirit?
Where are you?

Go ahead. It's okay.
Answer the call.
Allow each peculiar limitation
to lead you recklessly
into the arms
of a crazy-about-you
Lover.

Show your weakness.
Be received.
You are accepted
as
you
are.

QUEENDOM WITHIN

I remember you —
maybe from another lifetime
or story-thread
where kings and queens lived,
and jesters spoke their splendid truth.

You were there —
at the place where edgy earth
peeked from waters below.
Your form seemed to float
on the slippery slope of slate
as you gazed upon me with patience
and found my fins had faded
from faint promises I followed.

It's true—
I hadn't recognized the majesty of my being,
how the very king, queen and jester
from ancient lore lived within;
the quadrant community
of father, mother, spirit, child
were knitted in my very core.

And, you —
returned daily, without fail,
to call to me,
          Return, return.

I'll admit, I didn't hear your persistent barking for some time.
It was easier to ignore your giant eyes of love,
to carry on with the belief that I held an innate flaw and
someone else held the key I needed
to claim my sovereignty.

Here I am now—
in gratitude.
Thank you for not giving up on me.
For calling out —
          Return, return!
urging me to turn back
to the sealskin of myself,
where a reef of living color bubbles.

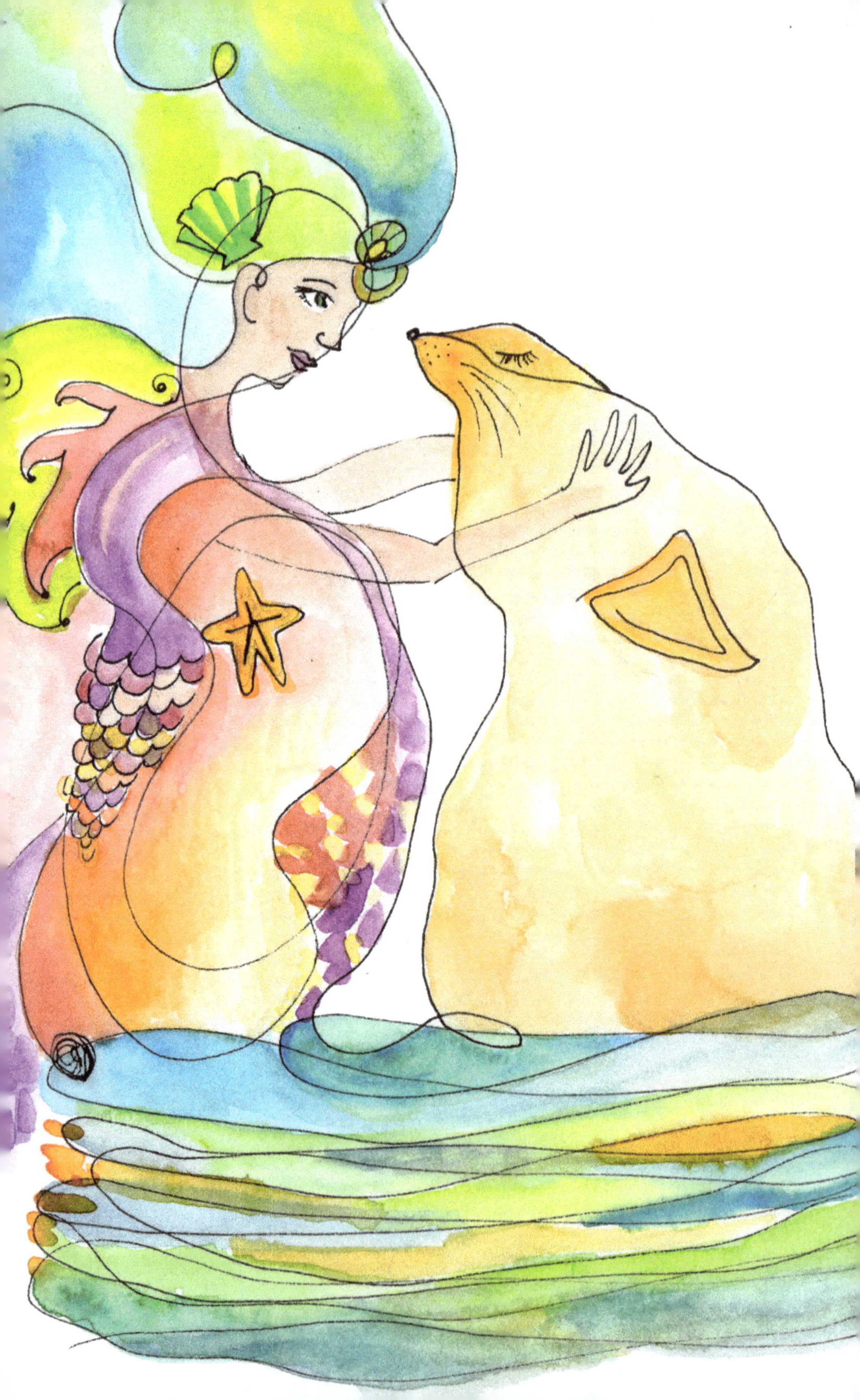

Today
I claim both the fins and the feet,
the inward dive and the starry stretch.

I am at home again,
in the majesty
of me, as creator
of my inner queendom.

NO TIME TO LOSE

The water draws me to her edge.
There I am, to soothe the sting.
I look in the abyss for a sign.
Tranquil hush stares back at me.
What do you see?, says the sea.
The truth is, it's only me.
Then I hear, *Love all of her.*
I dive into uncharted waters.
Make a wave, or two, or three.
The next day, I return.
And plunge again. And again.
Days turn to months turn
to seasons turn to years.
I learn to love the me I see.
All of her — splash and soul.
This practice of submerging
and emerging has me
soaking wet and amused.
Droplets drip and urge,
Share the good news.
I reach to the masses,
open hands and heart true:
There's no time to lose,
love all of YOU.

THE GARDENER

I wake at 7:16 a.m.
and decide I matter.
On this very day,
I choose to love myself.
I bend my ear to the
soft, ripe seed within me
rather than the voices that
promise a plan for my life.
My fingers sink
into cosmic astral pockets
and take hold of the magic
that belongs to me.
I toss my starry
sprinkle of balm
wherever I go —
and before long,
a garden flourishes
around me.
Flowers of fancies
keep arising.
Tell me,
what can I do other than
gather flowers and share them
with friends?

This ongoing beauty
guides me to nurture
the spiraling love within.
I regularly catch
sight of the gardener
who proclaims my name and speaks,
Keep growing. I am with you.
I do the only thing I can.
I keep growing.
And glowing.

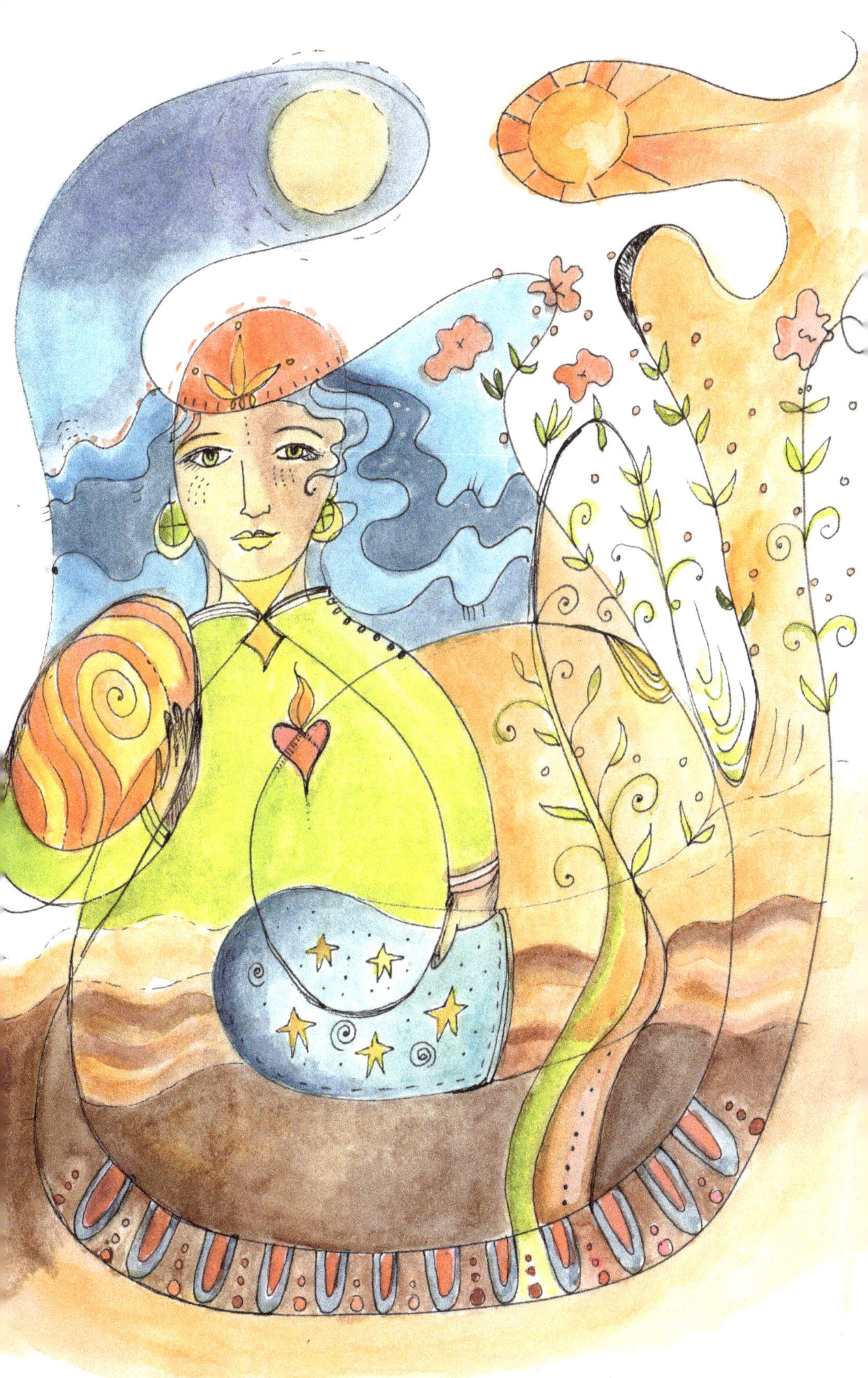

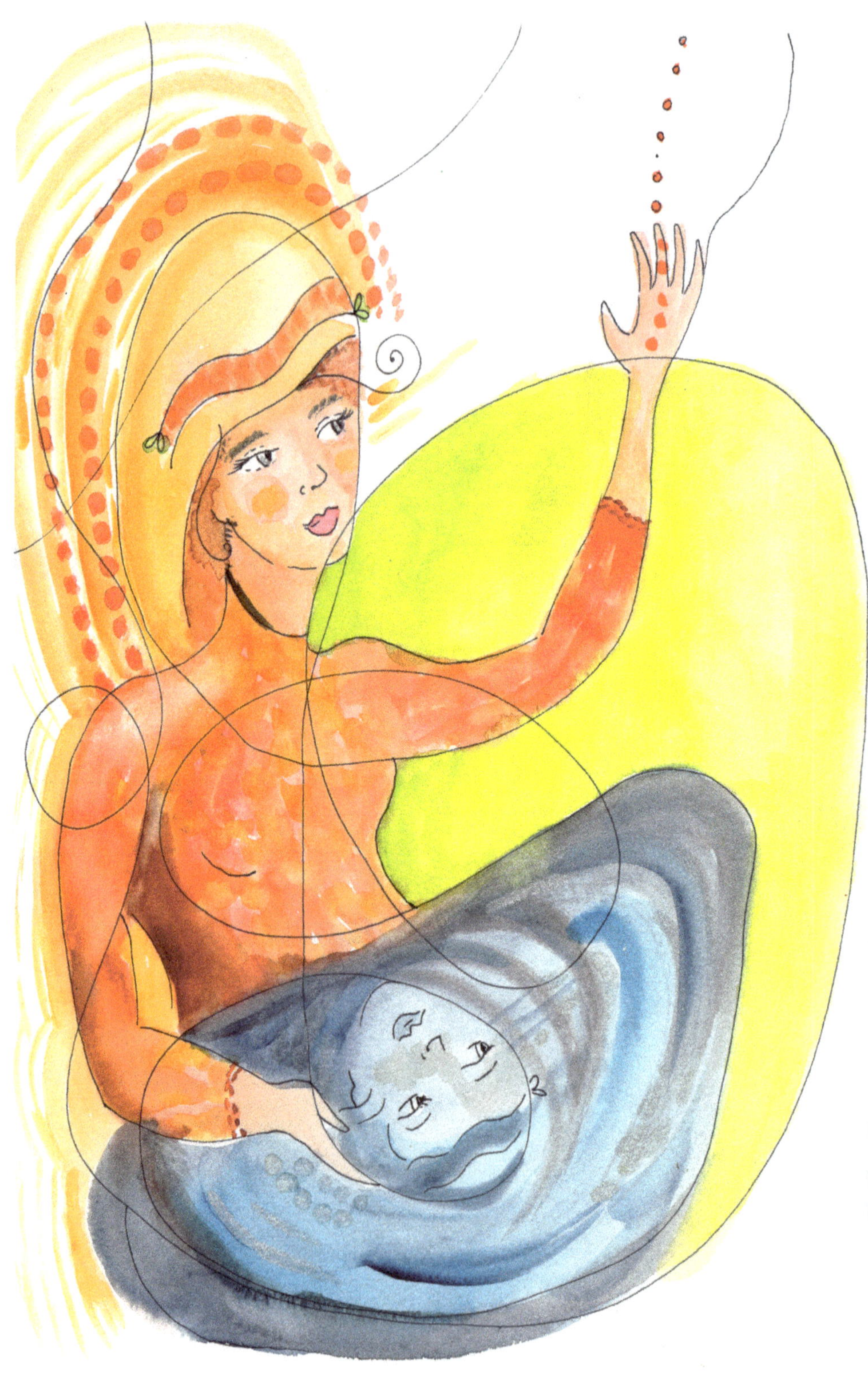

Who are you now
that you have asked
this question of becoming?

Who are you now
that you've received Love
from a Source beyond you, within you?

Who are you now
that you've taken your pencil
to write your story, your way?

Who are you now
that your heart dares
to discover your color and find your voice?

Who are you now
that you've said, *Yes,*
to show up to creative practice?

Who are you now
that you remember
the creative, sacred spark
that has been in you
since the beginning?

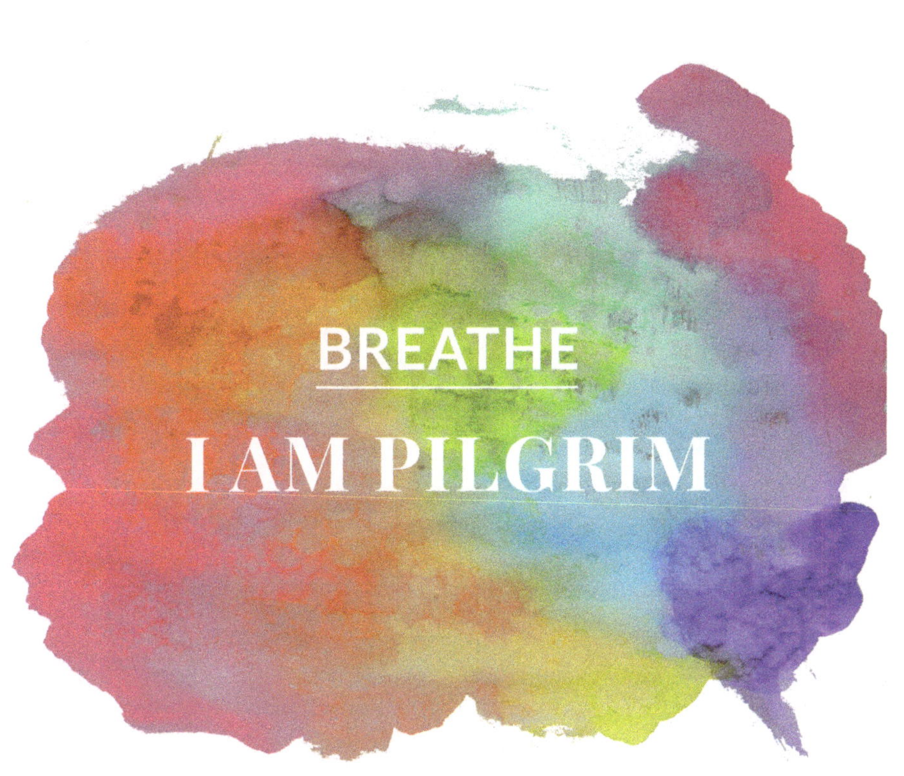

Refreshment for the
Midnight Trail

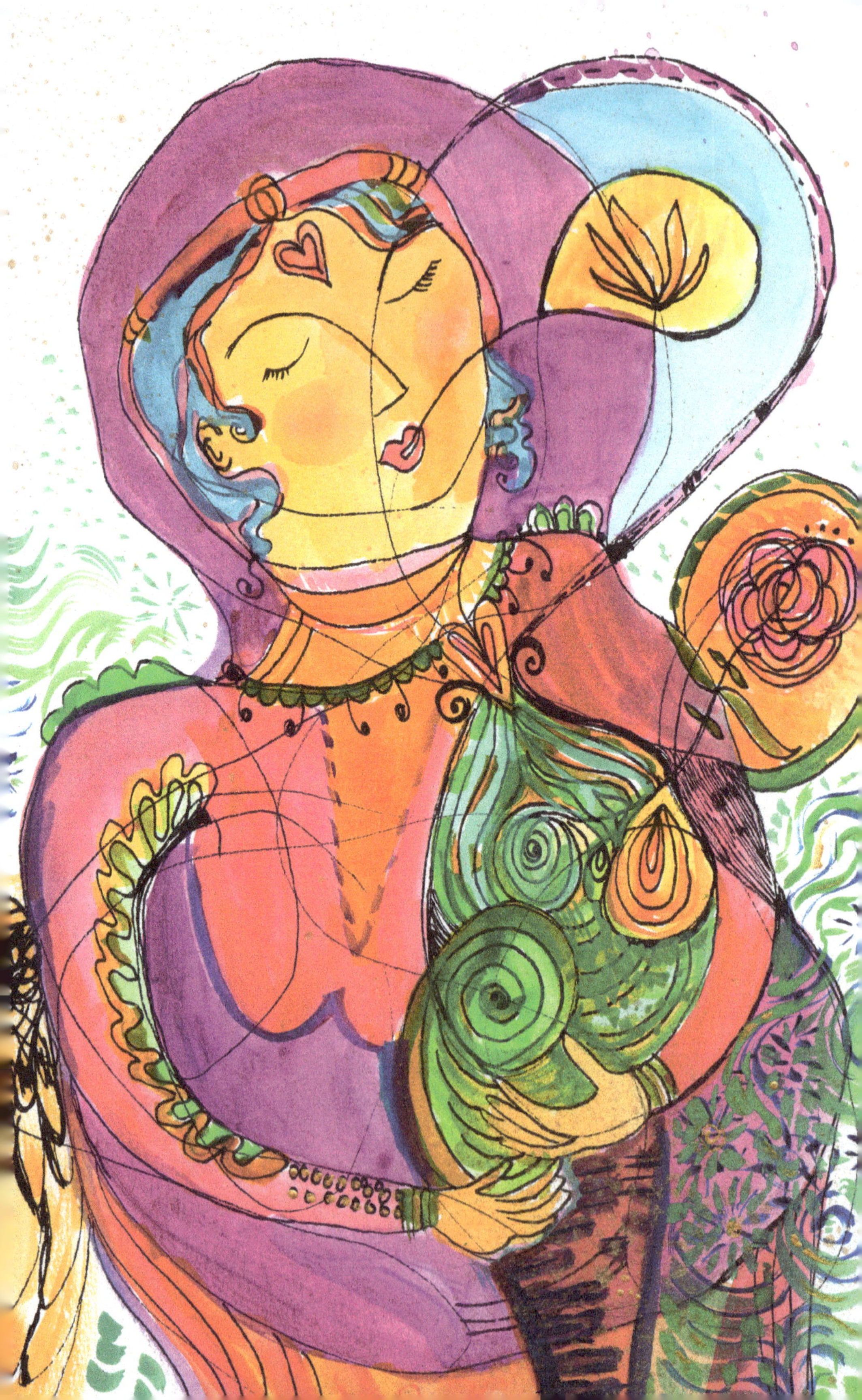

SPIRITED VOYAGER

Others may look at you
and note an ordinary woman.
But, you know better than that.
You sense the
fire in your veins,
feel breeze of vitality
in your lungs.
You trust your
sight for celestial details,
an inward expanse of stars
that stretch your sinews.
You've battled the waves
and let them
move you to their
pulsation of grace.

You are the
spirited voyager.

You are the one
who takes all
that has come,
gathers it
into a bundle
and answers the
imperative question,
*What can I do with
this hodgepodge of a story?*
You are certain nothing goes to waste.
You sew and you glue,
you paint and you glitter,
you scrub and you laugh.
You tend to the ordinary,
listening for the winds
that lean in close and
say, *This way.*
Then, you take your
rainbow tale
and you walk on.
You cross the bridge
of your reckoning.
You thank the grief and
claim the goodness and
step again toward
risky adventure.

The heart of mystery is
what you serve.

WHEEL OF LIFE

The wheel of life
never stops whirling goodness.
Her mercy is there for you
as sure as yellow lilies
rouse their friendly faces in spring.
All there is to do
is allow her compassion to brush up
against your dry bones,
plant atoms of luminosity within you
and WHOOSH —
the vine of vigor
begins her crawl,
a delicate bend from
hand to heart to voice
sprouting visions as
she goes.
Before long,
one of these has wings
and desires to fly.
Who are you to hold her back?
As this notion
was freely given,
you, inspired jewel,
open hands
and freely share.
As you do,
much to your astonishment
your own wings unfurl and expand.
You glide on the wind for the first time.

IS IT I?

Search for the genuine,
seek the true —
Is it I?
Is it you?

Keen like Goldilocks,
fish for clues —
I'm a spy;
join my crew?

Hug the art-of-be,

release the "do" —
Savor pie,
Ballyhoo!

False masks descend,
conceal their *Boo!* —
Who am I?
Come unglued.

Learn of La Loba,
lost bones her brew —
She tends my cry,
sings to imbue.

Toes in earth-sienna,
Eyes on sky-blue —
Here am I,
where are you?

Study raven medicine,
hear owl's, *Who* —
I can fly,
bid adieu.

Head toward the rainbow,
who with all her hues —
Vows to welcome,
expands the view.

Feel it in my heart
tingles the cue —
Love is wide,
never subdued.

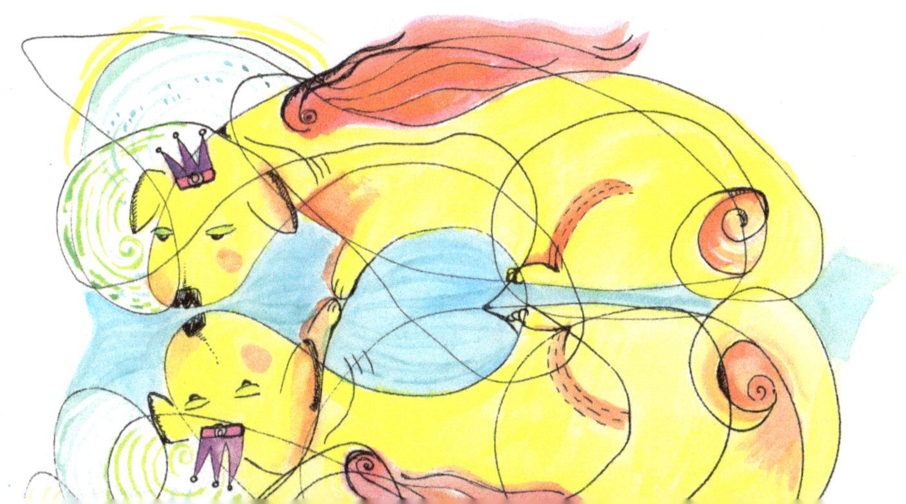

THE LITTLE GIRL OF MUD PIES

You were told not to get dirty.
Keep your fingernails clean.
Nice girls smile politely.
And, for goodness' sake,
Do not cuss!
But, you couldn't help to
bend your childlike knees
in your striped yellow dress,
leaning low toward the earth to
make a prayer with the loose soil
that lay beneath your feet.
You scooped handfuls of water and dust,
let wet mud mush between
your fingers; all this ooze
made you happy.
Slop. plop. slop.
Piles of plop added in rusty pie tins.
You, an artisan of mud pies.

You marched into the woods on a hunt for lions,
only to find their essence lurked behind willow trees.
You returned wiser, turning into a scholar of
that which you search for, you just may find.
This sent you on an expedition of liquids
that live in hidden cabinets –
pungent nectar for homemade magic potion.
Not much needed to make it happen.
Some ordinary water, mom's perfume,
a sprinkle of cleaning powder
and a few dandelion buds added.
You gave it a deliberate stir with a tree branch, and: *Ta da!*
This homemade alchemy made you suspect
that the power was within you.
And, it was.

You traded your pretty dress for jeans and t-shirts.
Like it or not, you took up cussing, because
you had this emotional volcano inside
ready to erupt. No-one told you:
add it to the end of your paintbrush,
move it through charcoal onto paper,
take a pencil and scribble it.
Maybe *they* weren't ready to accept the truth of you;
maybe *you* weren't ready to accept the truth of you.
Not that you blame anyone –

I mean how would they know to tell you creativity is a transformer
when it's been treated like a distracting hobby
best suited to make sweet crafty things?

The emotions. The moods.
It came from a propensity to perceive the heartache
within and around you —
a grieving you thought you needed to wear.
You wore all of it on your shoulders as a shawl of mourning.
Maybe if you garbed yourself in it, they would get a glimpse.

You searched for Love and soon enough
you heard a fierce and gentle Divine voice say, "Follow me."
You felt tingles, and you loved love, so you went.
This route felt different than the one
you'd traveled before. It was healthier.
More hopeful. And, there was lots to learn.
Over time, you were swept up in the intellect,
losing the little girl of mud pies
as you traded imagination for knowledge.
Your gut told you there was something different.
more authentic. tastier. real.
your thirst was for the living. The LIVING!
You noted the story of Christ
who embodied this effervescence.
Christ wasn't boring —
but held wisdom in the mystical realm,
treasures for those who dwell at His/Her feet.

You did the only thing you could do:
You started an investigation:
Question after question —
about other faiths. and practices.
You questioned authority. tradition. erected walls.
You asked where MotherGod is
and why She remained in the background.

It's not that you got the "right" answers
to any of these inquiries. But,
this inspection led you right back —
to the mud pies with dirty fingernails.
To what you learned when you were five:

All the colors and flavors of the rainbow belong.
Play is good for the soul. Treat each other with kindness.
Jesus loves you (so does Mother Mary).
—*This you know.*

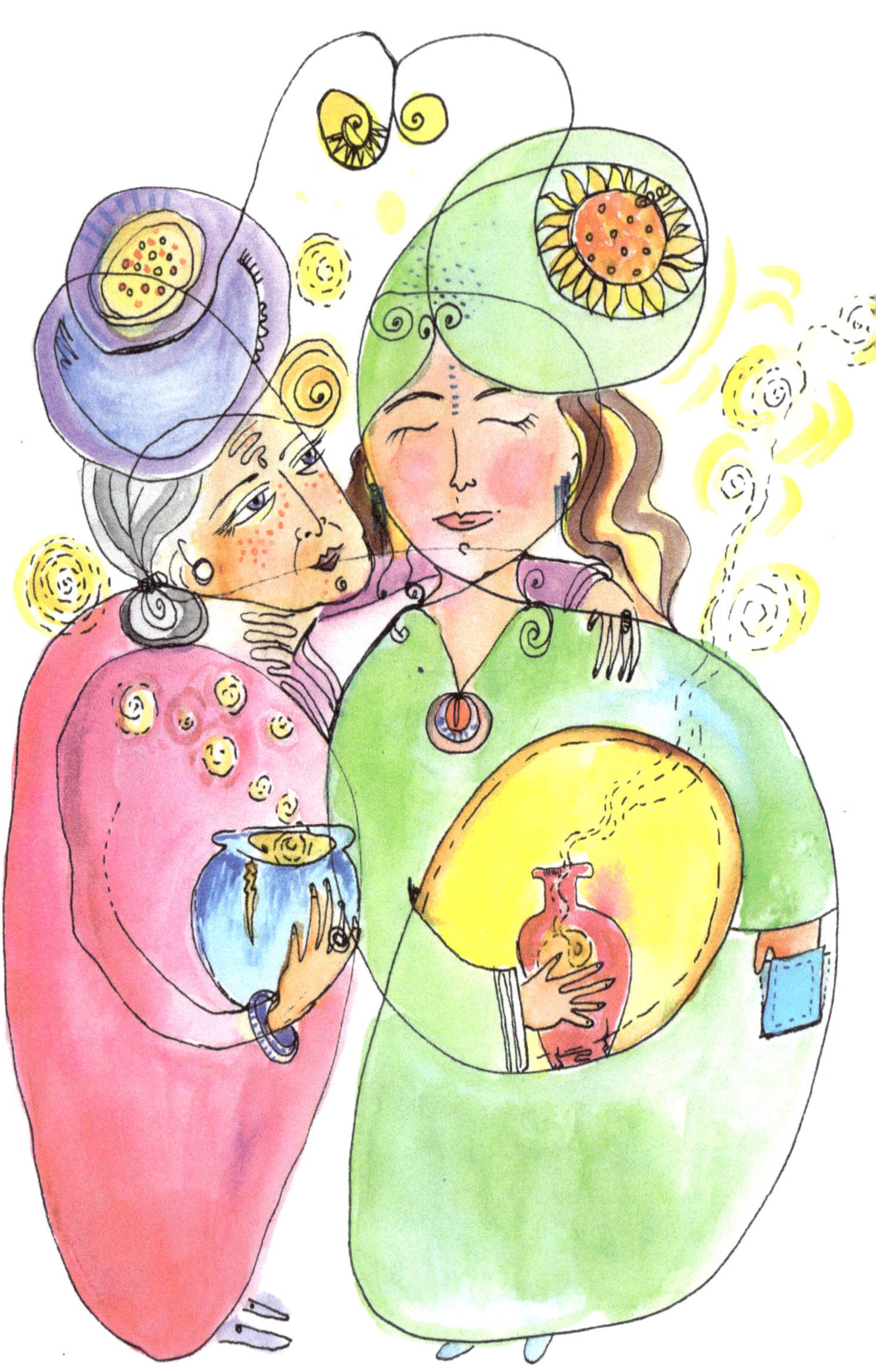

This recovered teaching took you back to the studio —
to make a clay dragon pinch pot.
You donned a stripe of wet earth on your brow
as you molded red clay.
As you kneaded, you found healing.
You came to understand the fragility of creation,
how at any point it can lose structure —
be dropped, cracked, broken.
You came to see —
everything is impermanent.
The act of creation is a snapshot of the present.
The magic IS the making.

The old voices attempted to bellow,
Now, don't make a mess.
Don't get too excited!
And, for goodness' sake,
Do not use glitter!

But, you knew better.
You took the glitter out and shook it high.
It flew into all the crevices of the room,
covered your hair with golden abundance,
flecks of light raining on your neighbor,
a crunch of silver in your mouth.

Flutter of confetti
let you loosen your grip. Your grit.
Here. In this clay sanctuary
you learned mud carries an epiphany.
And so does glitter.

This time,
you chose to celebrate the grit
and wear the glitter.

Good choice.
'cause, girl —
glitter sure looks good on you.

DESPITE CAUTIONARY TALES, MY SANITY AT RISK

I've decided to follow beauty —
precious treasure of the beholder's eye

I've decided to follow the trail of the squirrel —
playful scamperer of green-branch habitat

I've decided to follow smoke of the sage —
earthy scent of adoration

I've decided to follow curl of the wind —
gentle nudge of watery ripples

I've decided to follow cycle of the moon —
cosmic smile of wax and wane

I've decided to follow flame of the fire —
arms of warmth for weary seekers

I've decided to follow rivers of plenty —
where division is less, inclusion is more

I've decided to follow Mother herself —
clever cavity of cadence and Christ

I've decided to follow passion of the heart —
passage of peace in a spinning world

Despite cautionary tales,
your sanity at risk:

What have you decided to follow?

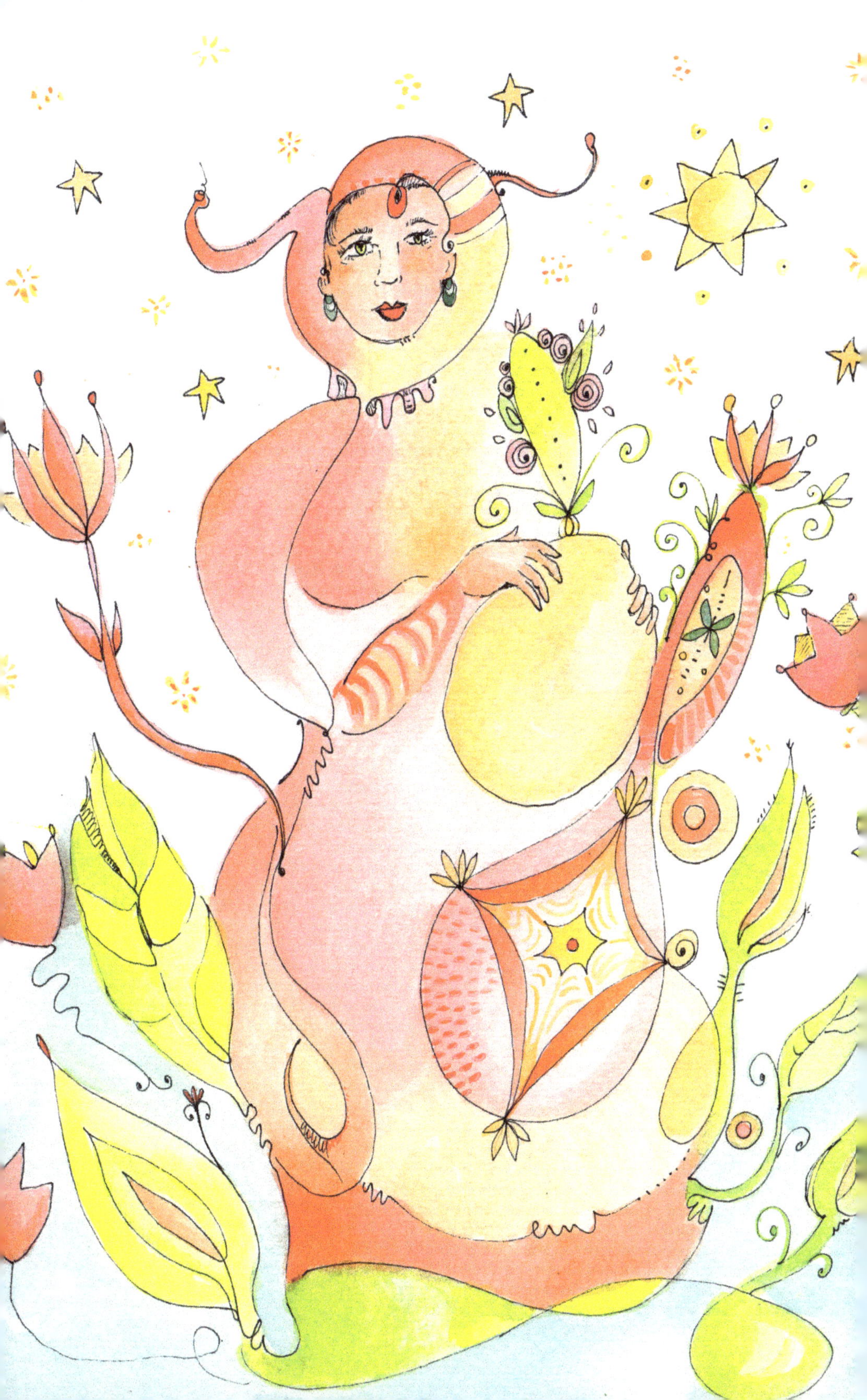

THE SPIRAL PATH

Artist.
Poet.
Contemplative.
Feminist.
Mystic.

From your first inhale,
a spark is born:

Colors are joy.
Letters are magic.
Silence is sacred.
Women matter.
You matter.
Prayer is real.

The path of the dreamer isn't linear —
your steps are an ongoing spiral.
An ocean of detail swirls within,
routine wonder informs the work.

Around here, silence is kept.
Language lets loose as
color washes,
symbol swashes,
justice prayers,
mysterious stares

Visual expression reveals
tender shoots of emotional growth.

You are born —
again, and
again, and
again

as you create from the diamond
of your thoughtful vigilance.

This silent language is available to you,
yet spoken words, written words
seem to fill every crack.

Solitude purrs your name.

You aren't "busy" crafting,
twiddling your thumbs with a "hobby."

You are uncoiling the nitty gritty,
getting real with the complex colors of being.

As you make,
you merge into creator AND observer.

What you conceive entices you to pay attention:

What glides with ease?
What rubs with discomfort?

Your personal seas churn,
you abide their quake until they pass.

You wield your mythic paint brush,
novel shapes rise, declare a view of peace.

You show up to yourself,
color your cravings into reality —
again, and
again, and
again.

Amen.

WHILE YOU WAIT

You,
girl of the ocean,
swimmer of the sea,
washed up ashore,
displaced at the heart of your honesty.
And, now —
you, the ever curious one, ponder,
What do I do
while I wait?

Well, dear one,
as the dry air rushes past,
nearly knocking you down,

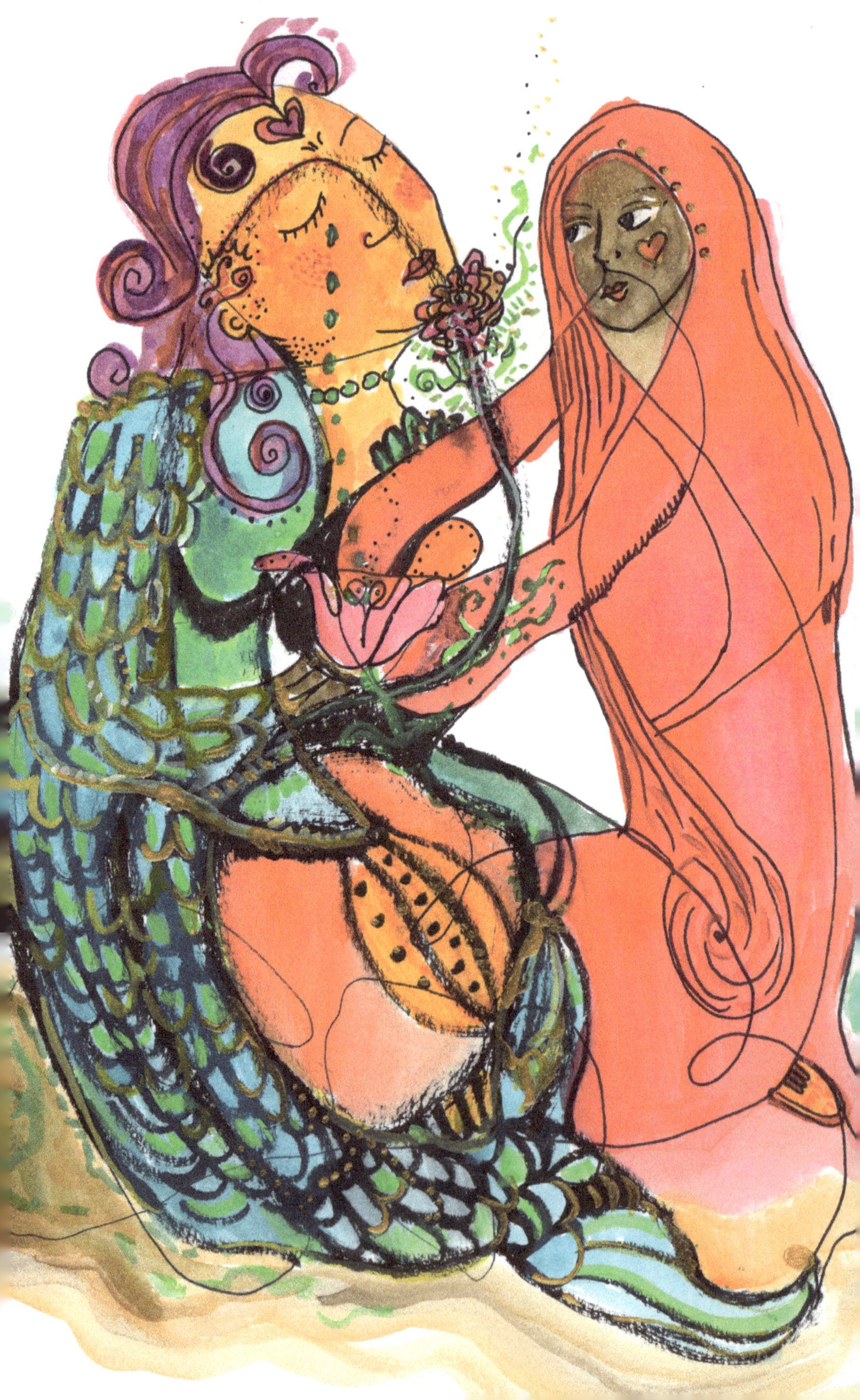

let the tears fall
and nourish what you hold.

You,
caretaker of creation,
keeper of the flame,
bearer of truth,
whatever you do — don't rush it.
Really.

Allow the space
of emptiness to hold you.
Listen. Hear that?
A lullaby from
your deep-seated essence
whooshing you to sleep—
inklings and insights
laid on your heart.

What you don't glimpse
are clandestine threads
strung together,
cords of love weaving you
into a greater story,
a story you may
never understand
yet will enfold you in mercy.

While you wait,
please know *(know)* —
there is one
on bended knee
holding your hand,
wiping your tears.

She is for you.
You are not alone.

INTO THE MIDNIGHT HOUR

Shady black rolls into town —
comes as clouds of gloom
that infiltrate the space.

This story begins with the line,
On a dark and stormy night;
its an ancient yarn shared —
one you may have heard before:
death is the central point.

When this tale is told,
a dappled blue fog of grief descends,
lures you toward
a grim alleyway of lostness
where black is on trial.

Of all the hues, you see—
black is the edgy one;
it's identity has been up in the air for some time —
Is it all pigments mixed together
or the absence of light?

This confusion has turned black into
a shade to fear, associated with the negative.

Now is the time to recover darkness
from its sordid reputation.
Where can we go to
learn the treasures of soot
and soil, of dirt and mud?
There is one named
the Black Madonna —
whose presence calls us to
pay respect to clouded infinity —
She cradles jewels of the earth
and asks us to navigate our depths.

Only the courageous search for Her…

Even She has been whitewashed,
her story a bleached tale of candle smoke.

For ages,
we have been taught
to view darkness as evil

and narrow MotherGod's goodness
to all light.

In this we delete the pain
and the woman who bore
the divine child.

Isn't the deep abyss
where life begins?
Don't the rich tiers
of clay, sand, and soil
hold secrets for how
seedlings sprout forth their beauty?

Just imagine —
you are this seed of becoming.
It's time to listen for secrets of the night.

Lamps are off. Your eyes are wide
in the dark depths of stillness.
Soul stirs. Mind plays games.
Fingers drum.
Seems like nothing is happening here
in this smoky space.
Black drips like honey —
this drizzle directs you to pause your judgments
and stretch your fingers toward
your heart in tenderness.

In this faded ebony-rest,
a visitor knocks on your door —
to shift the furniture of your soul.

A veil falls over your inner sheen
to remind you that life isn't linear —
but a spiral adventure that
whirls us into a great gala of becoming.

In this twirling —

Do you reach for the Parent of soothing compassion?
Mama — see me, nurture me, hold me!
Do you reach for the Parent of sacred grace?
Abba — forgive me for I know not what I do!

When you stroll with the black cat,
and hear her purr,
the categories of good and bad dissolve,

shadows and light play together;
sensations buzz
in the cave of transformation.

This *aha!* awakens your womb space
and new life begins to form.

When worry arrives at midnight,
you choose to wake bleary-eyed,
burn a candle for your secret shadow,
and listen to your heart-hum.
Then, you lay out a pillow and say,
There, there
and let your worries dream.

As dawn breaks through mist,
a rainbow arcs,
falling in love is alive — You
pray pigments are released
from harsh criticism.

From this earthy haven
a sturdiness spreads,
a firm trunk forms;
your branches stretch.
The bud of giving cracks open,
flavorful fruit comes forth.

You discover you aren't alone;
you stand in a grove with others.
You and I are co-creators
blowing our breeze,
sowing seeds as we go:
Yes!
Mother of the Living is here.
We are a vital part of
Her Queendom on earth.

The world is held by dark and light. And,
what you thought looked hopeless
is, in fact, the tree of life whose roots
go deep and ground you on your way.
It is here where you embrace your shadows.
It is here where you claim the wholeness of you,
your eyes born again to the incarnate love
that is found within.

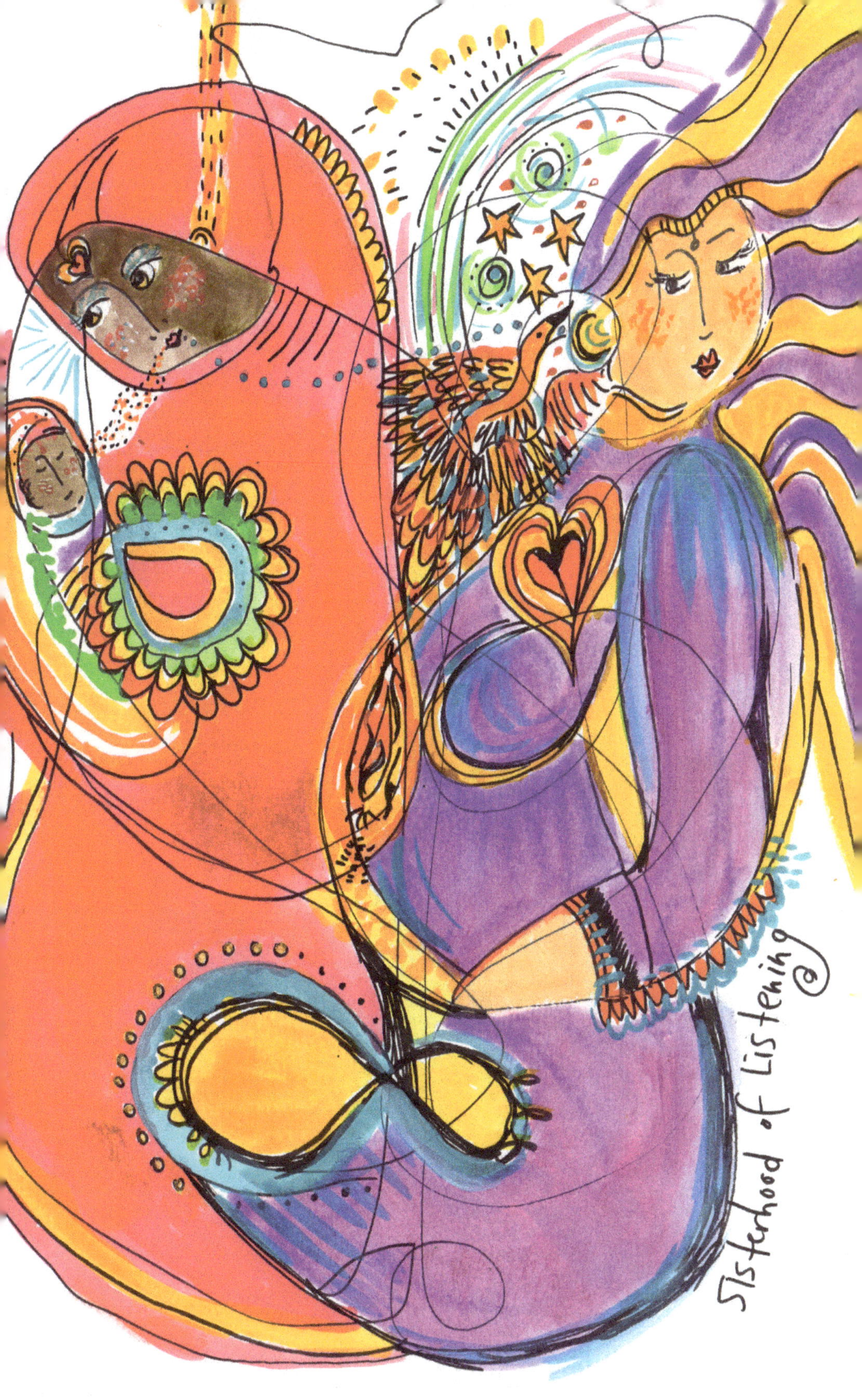

Sisterhood of Listening

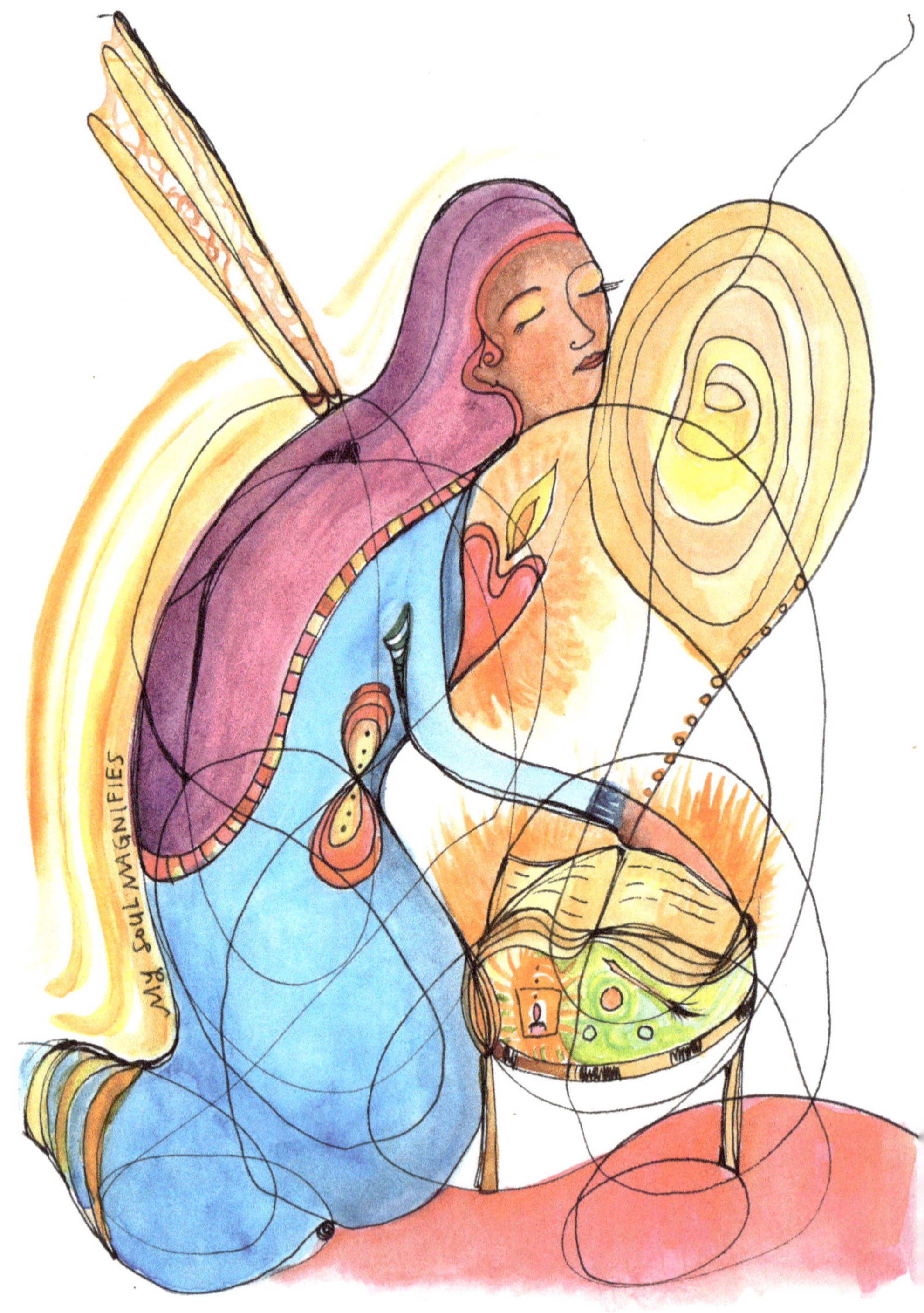

My Soul Magnifies

SEEKER OF ASH

I'm drained
from petitions to
pursue the Light —
eyes on the prize
of risen joy.

As if
the light
is the only thing
I need
to seek,
and it's

here.

No. (there.)

Just. out. of. reach.

Separate from me.

I try to grasp it.
Arms outstretched.
But
fingers
can't
reach the
blaze.

I fall on my knees.

Exhausted
from trying.

Overhead,
silver fingers wisp in the sky;
they point to the ground.

I take my fingers
and press them into soft soil,
move them through blades of grass —
dirt finds my fingernails;
I dig instinctively.

Soon enough,
I'm elbow-deep
in faint memories
laced with red oxide
and healing powers.

Holy richness rises
from the black abyss,
reverence of the rayless dark.
I lean in and listen;
a buzz of forgotten stories reach me,
tales buried under twisted roots
release their seeds.

I stand woozy from what I've uncovered.
My legs carry me to ancient pages
to search for confirmation
of what I've found.

The black text is a clue.
I become a detective.

I pull my magnifying glass out
and peruse the space between letters;
inspect the empty places only few
are brave enough to speak about.

I find an age-old thread.

This golden strand leads me to
the basement of the cathedral.
Here, lost, sacred stories reside
behind secret doors.
I knock three times
and the doors swing slowly ajar.
I see a path lit by torches; I follow
the glow to an immense bookcase.

From a high shelf, I gently pull
one volume down and, sitting,
place it on my lap.
I dust off the cover.
Hazy ash fills the air.

I crack the spine open
to a lightning bolt revelation:
*Wisdom has been here
since the beginning.*

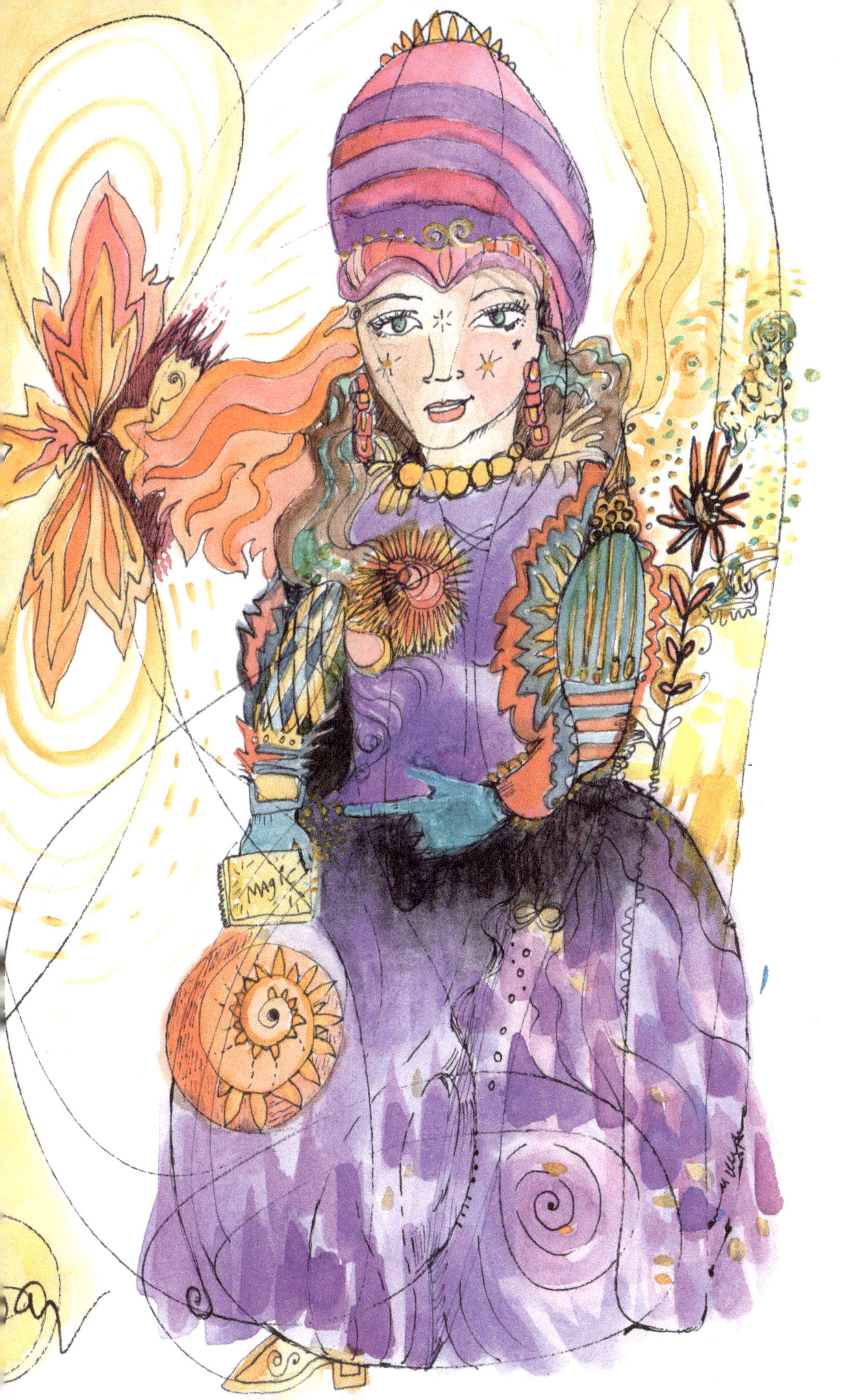

Wisdom is a She.
The way She has been covered up
breaks my heart open.
I weep for all that's been concealed;
and brim with rising joy
for what I'm finding. . .

ARE YOU COMING?

Outside,
the moon gazes with grace.

Inside,
I crouch in the basement of the cathedral,
rifle through the relic on my lap,
flashlight in hand, flip with fury,
find forgotten details.

Crrrrrreeeeeak, crrrrrreeeeeak, crrrrrreeeeeak
Hearing footsteps above me,
my heart stops—
What if they find me?

Quiet settles, I keep on,
forge for Wisdom
on the wily way.

With eyes on coiled wisdom, there She is —
legs stretch toward awareness,
to face the fable of sin:
Eve, forager of solid food.

With fluid connection, there She is—
hands embrace a duffel of fragility,
treasure in lap,
Rachel, bearer of code.

With air of knowledge, there She is—
mouth speaks of sacred Spirit
teaches freely in the chosen circle,
Magdalene, confidant of Christ.

By now, my eyes fling open
to ancient women as prophets of moxie
whose true stories have been stifled.
Spirit blows in,

calling herself Sophia;
her torch ignites ghost stories.
She affirms my discovery.

She unrolls blueprints —
shows fingerprints found on tambourines,
messages filtered through reed baskets,
bottles filled with healing balm.

I place the holy treasure on the floor,
race to tell the others.
I weave through cobwebs,
face my own midnight fear.

With rigid gait, there they are—
minds fierce with intellect,
brains fastened to fact.
Columns of structure, faces of uniformity.

When I mention —
Feminine Grace
Wisdom at the Fountain
Lady of Breath
they reel their heads back,
peel with laughter —

My voice is stifled by their disdain —
I plead for perception to awaken, beg
for creative incense to lead us beyond conformity.
My soft words stir a memory in them.

The pillars remember a time
when women elders made a scene —
when they banged drums
for Lady Divine to be admitted
into the sanctuary.
The faces of uniformity couldn't imagine,
they held firm — She was shut out,
doors closed to her presence.

I stutter and flutter.
But when? Why?
How can Divinity be a male-only club?
The towers shrug, uninterested.

Wind of Grace catches my nose.

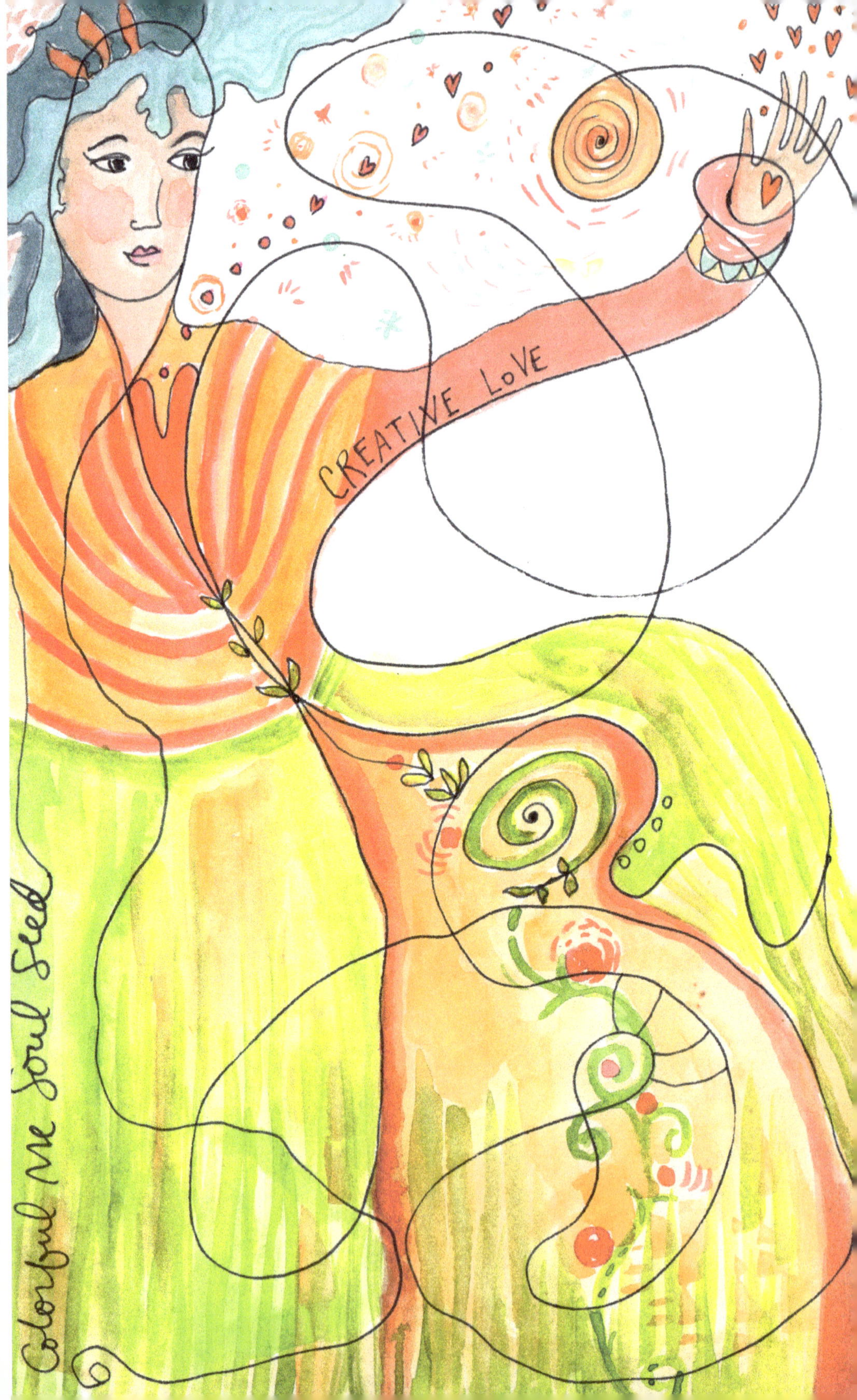

CREATIVE LoVE
Colorful me Soul Seed

A fox on the scent,
I dart past the columns with flair.
I hear a celebration, a reckoning.
I tiptoe into the night and find —

prophetesses
artists
activists
seekers

For these are the fugitives
who carry the hidden stories,
they press their voice
out to the rim of the galaxy,
their echo rings true.

This is where the thread is passed
to the next generation
for change to be made.

They yell to me with passion, *Are you coming?*
I run to the band of merry mystic-makers
to march to their fresh song:
Pass the thread, pass the thread, Ooooo, *la la*

What about you?
Are you coming?

THE MOONLIT PATH

There I stand in the pulpit —
I preach of healing grace.
I try not to get my hands dirty, but
the confined, holy habit unleashes.
Dualistic concepts collide,
shadow urges to claim Her piece of holy.

Sleep comes easily as evening descends,
the moon lit with a whisper.
Soul warriors polish Luna gently,
crafting precious work, laying seeds of love.
I find protection as the howl
of the wolf is placed in my gut.

Outside the church entry,
atoms of ash gleam in open air.
Leaves shimmer from breezy trees,
stardust drifts through the skies.
Holy goodness streams boundlessly.
My world shifts to color,
images of collaboration begin to dance.

Awakening, my body sails,
as I reckon Spirit is HERE.
She flies over walls
into the outdoor sanctuary.
I burst with growing excitement.
My desire to give shape to this cannot be held any longer.
Words come to birth and colors swell
in their radiant unfolding,
My hands race to tell the tale.

Soon, a song of love opens within me,
lyrical nectar flows through my body —
I encounter her familiar warmth,
name Her Soul Mama;
I remember Her from long ago —
Her vibration radiates tranquil truth;
She hums sweet, blessed freedom.

My loneliness begins to give way as I embark
on the ancient road of my ancestors.
I gently release chains of status
and the "get-it-done" beat that has bound me.
I start to move forward untethered,
received fully into a dream of my own.

OPEN HANDS

Dear one,
I see you with your
hands clenched tight,
eyes twisted in pain,
the divine squeezed
to the size of a mustard seed,
nearly unable to breathe,
knotted up in
confusion and doubt,
your sense of the future uncertain.

You, beloved,
holding tight to the
reigns of control,
to they way things should be,
oughta be.
But, dear one,
(and I say this gently, with love) —
Nothing can ever,
(ever)
be received or given with
hands shut.
So then, beloved,
slow down and delight
in the divine seed
you hold in your hands.
Note the golden bit of goodness,
the living presence of Goddess.

Study its size,
feel its form,
observe its color.
This is the presence
of the sacred,
knitted within you.
Give thanks.
When the time is right
(and you'll know when it is),
allow your fingers to
break open. When you do,
a great release
of breath and tension
will overflow.
Then, all at once,
holy magic begins
to push away uncertainty,
and you receive and transmit
a brilliant shower of light
simultaneously.
This divine beam,
streaming into you,
flowing forth from you,
naturally bathes
the world with
the unique love
only you can provide.
Open your hands, beloved.
Open your heart.
(I believe in you.)

A FEAST AWAITS

I simmer in a stew of "busy,"
a star of importance pinned on my lapel.
This is the "success" culture sells, as you know.
The one who is most stressed, stretched thinnest, wins —
right?

The appeal for me comes in appearing composed
even as I quake within.

As Ru Paul says, *We're all born naked and the rest is drag.*
So, who is it I'll show up as?
Add some eye liner, rouge and a fuchsia scarf —
mere basics for one who dabbles with color daily.
By now, I'm adept at hiding under a garb of beauty
amid a sea of activity.

In midlife, without outfit or lipstick to cover me,
my well-woven tapestry begins to unravel
as I flash one final crowd-pleasing smile.

It's clear my essence is on strike
My intuitive antennae are alert to my deceit.
Something is "off."
The work of being "busy" drains me.
But I'm aware that depth pursues me.
I spot the sofa and her open arms.
I take a seat in her softness.

I quiet myself. I attune myself to the deep.
On a search for something beyond me, within me.
My mind wanders, I attempt to focus.
Not much happens.

Next afternoon. I arrive on the sofa again.
I, once again, practice finding that deep stillness.
I (inhale) Am (exhale). Again and again.

Nothing happens. But, this *nothing*
changes *everything.*
I sense MotherGod receives me
right there in my state of nothingness.
How does She love me if I'm not serving,
behaving good, gaining stripes for my lapel?

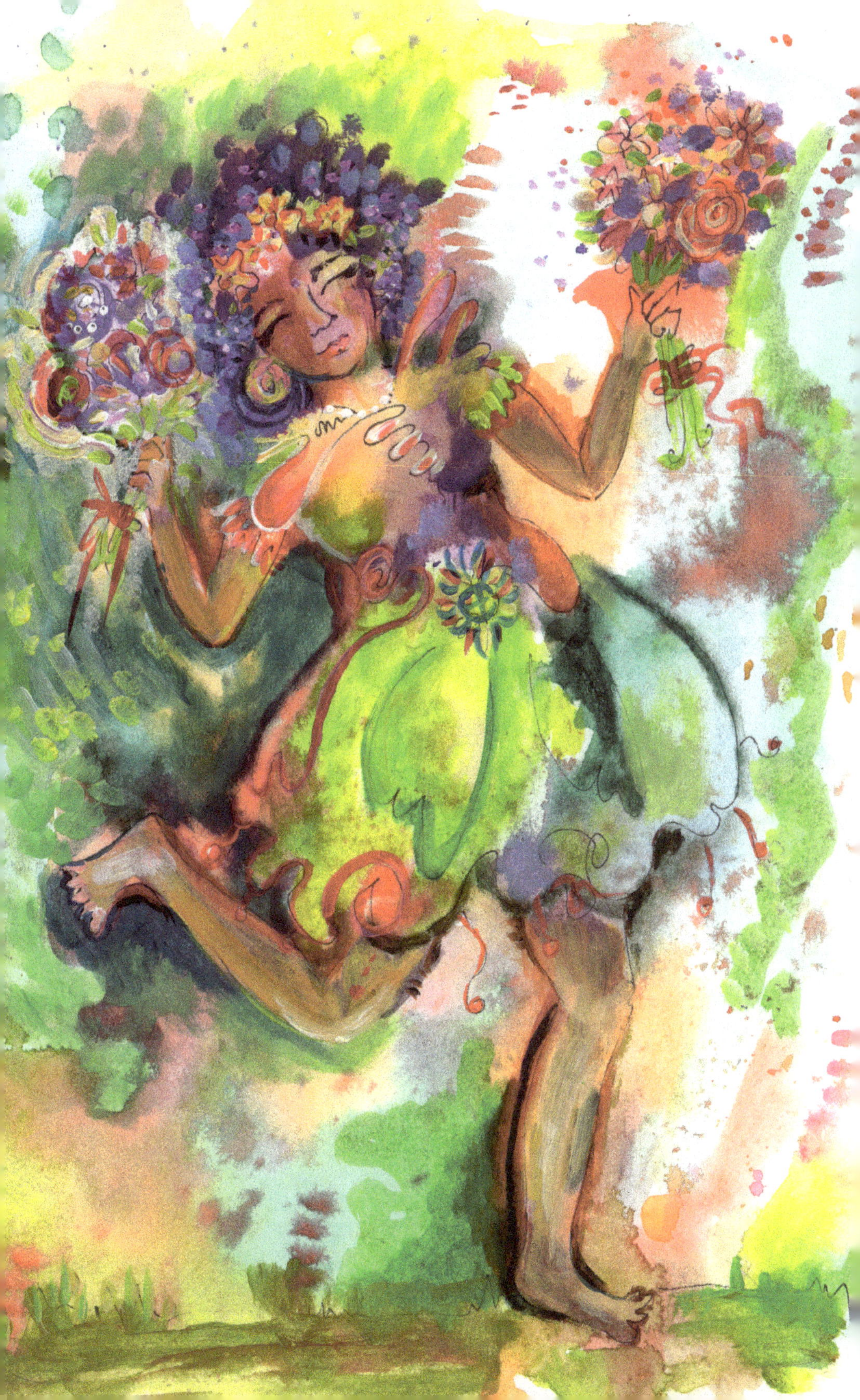

Because She is MotherGod
who births me.

The scales on my eyes slowly peel
to reveal the sacred in my midst.

As I let go, this is what I grasp:
MotherGod requests communion with me.
But I must still myself to be with Her.

I leap off the hamster wheel in a blaze of flailing glory.
It's not pretty.
I quit the roles I serve.
I say *No* to invitations.
Denying people isn't easy.
There is no simple exit.
I stumble in a daze out the door.
People seem afraid of the truth I am discovering.
I lose relationship with community.
The void greets me.

Still, I am drawn by the mystery.
Because MotherGod celebrates me
in my nothingness,
my pursuit of sacred Love intensifies.

The leap into the unknown
is somber for some time.
I pine for activity even while I curse it.
I wander aimlessly.
I begin to sense the presence of angels
who come to tend to me.

All this tests my trust. I step to the edge of potential.

A door opens. My heart leaps. My skin tingles.
I say *Yes* to the mysterious adventure
unfolding within me.
I envision the colors of my life
and realize that I am an artist. I begin anew.

Here, in this place of solace,
I find fellowship with the Artisan of my Soul.
A feast of creativity beckons. Every day.

I become the visionary pilgrim who
spirals from the center with lines of devotion.
The act of creating becomes my prayer.
As I trust showing up more fully,
the revelation unfolds within me.
I keep on opening to Her call.

The pilgrimage entices me forward.
My roots connect to the depths of Mother Earth,
my branches reach out into the horizon.
I commune with divinity in nature
and discover a sense of timelessness,
within and around me.

Now, I return to tell others of this incredible feast.
Here goes:
Darling one, there is a feast! A feast!
A communion where you can come as you are
(no pretending or acting required),
a homecoming to yourself.
Here, the Living Breath of Spirit awaits your presence,
to infuse you with grace and love.
All you have to do is be still
and open to Her coming.

Will you?
This communion
changes EVERYTHING.
Even *you.*

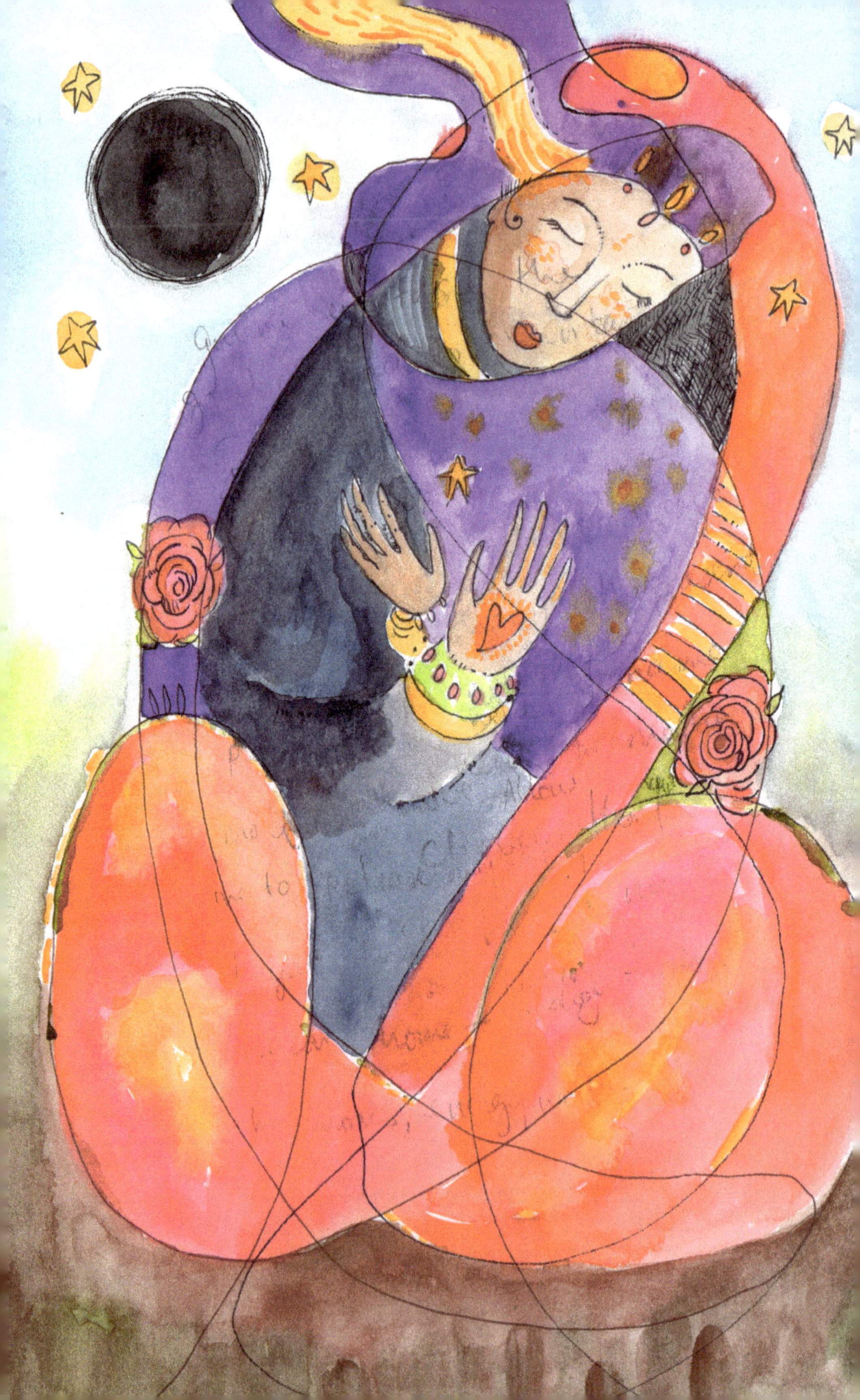

A POETIC REFLECTION ON *I AM PILGRIM*

You've traveled a long way, my friend.
You've navigated the depths with gentle compassion.
You've learned to embrace more than *the light.*

Now is a good time to pause.
To rest. To reflect.
For the sake of your body.
For the sake of your soul.
For the sake of your whole life.
Gather a marker or two or three.
Draw a windy road on a blank sheet.
Add the hills and mountains
you've had to cross.
Paint a valley line.
Add specks of joy along the path.
Puddle your blue grief as lakes of compassion.

Ask, *what else needs to be included?*
What is the name of this journey I've been on?

Gaze at the sacred map of your travels.
Give thanks for the whole.
Enjoy the fruits of your experience.
You've come so far.
It's time to celebrate YOU.

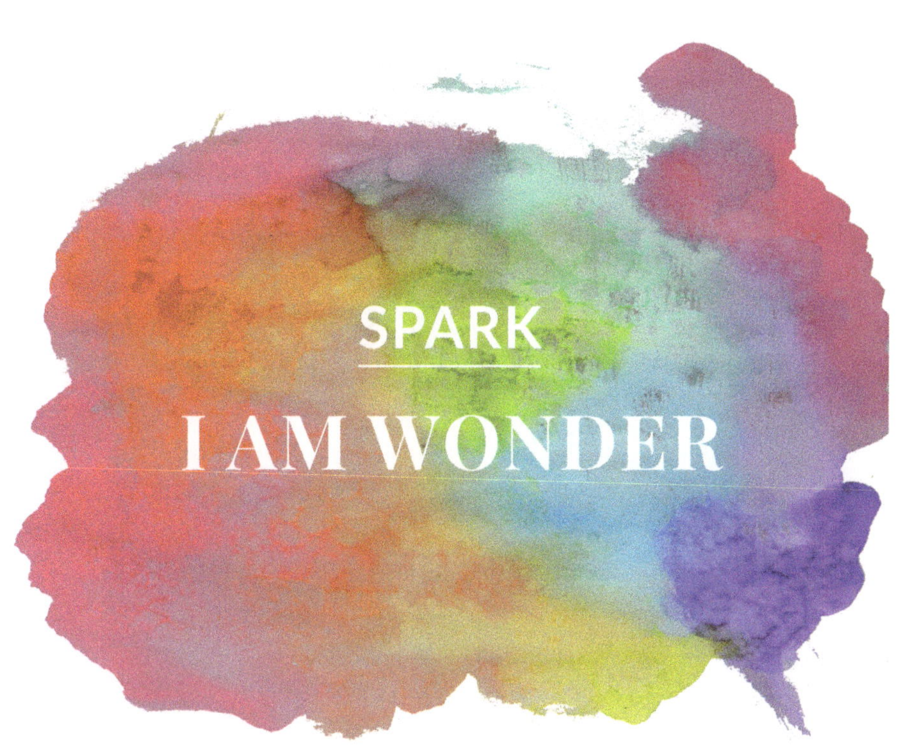

I AM WONDER

Ignite Possibility and
Sacred Imagination

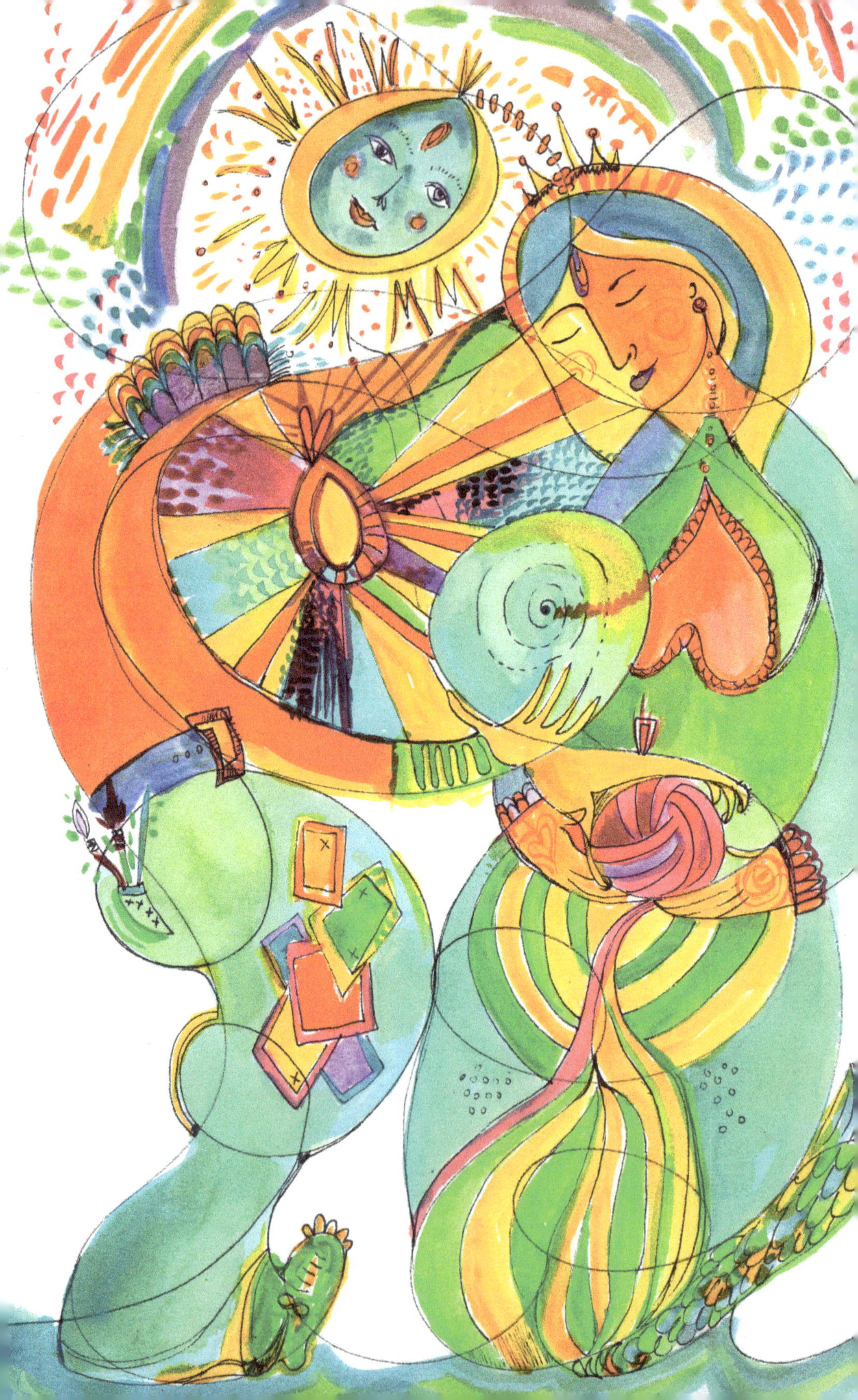

MAGIC'S GIFT

Dear Imagination,
I'm calling out to you,
not with chit-chat,
but with soul resonance,
sending you shimmery showings
of the innermost me
to woo your coming.

When I do,
there you are,
a rippling current of truth
opening from within.

Do you mind if I
use your nickname—
Magic?

(thank you)

Magic—
I follow the red thread you
have woven through my life
and attune to your prismatic presence.
Your words of invocation
wash over me, your
charm brings forth
an aspect of myself
I'd forgotten was mine.

I'm on my knees
to say, *I'm sorry,*
for the ways I've buried you
in the furthest corner of
my dusty closet,
for the stubborn tale of excuses
I concocted:
I don't have time for you.
My expression of you isn't good enough,
(maybe even),
I'm not worthy of you.

Remember how you helped me rewrite
the ending of *Romeo & Juliet*
with teenager lingo or that time

you conjured up a bedroom made
out of oodles of candy?

So good. So true. So beautiful.

My favorite of them all was
when you emboldened me
to pen a direct narrative
of my personal story,
possibly the most genuine work
I ever wrote
for others to read,
only to
have the door shut to my
vulnerable words.

Oh, the heartbreak.
Yet, I know I'm not alone.
Many of us have these
door closing moments
that lead us to believe,
   No, I'm not a writer.
   I'm not an artist.
   I'm not a creator.
tumbling, tumbling into
dangerous territory, the swamp
where others' assessment
determine your worth

Magic—
I'm here to express my gratitude.
Thank you for being here
when I was ready
to welcome you again.
Thank you for not giving
up on me. Instead, you do
what you do – come bearing
gifts that waft an aroma
that enlivens senses and
visualizes the stars.

You are the one who brings structure to
the void, tracking foolish dreams
to remote pastures.
This is the road of Magic.

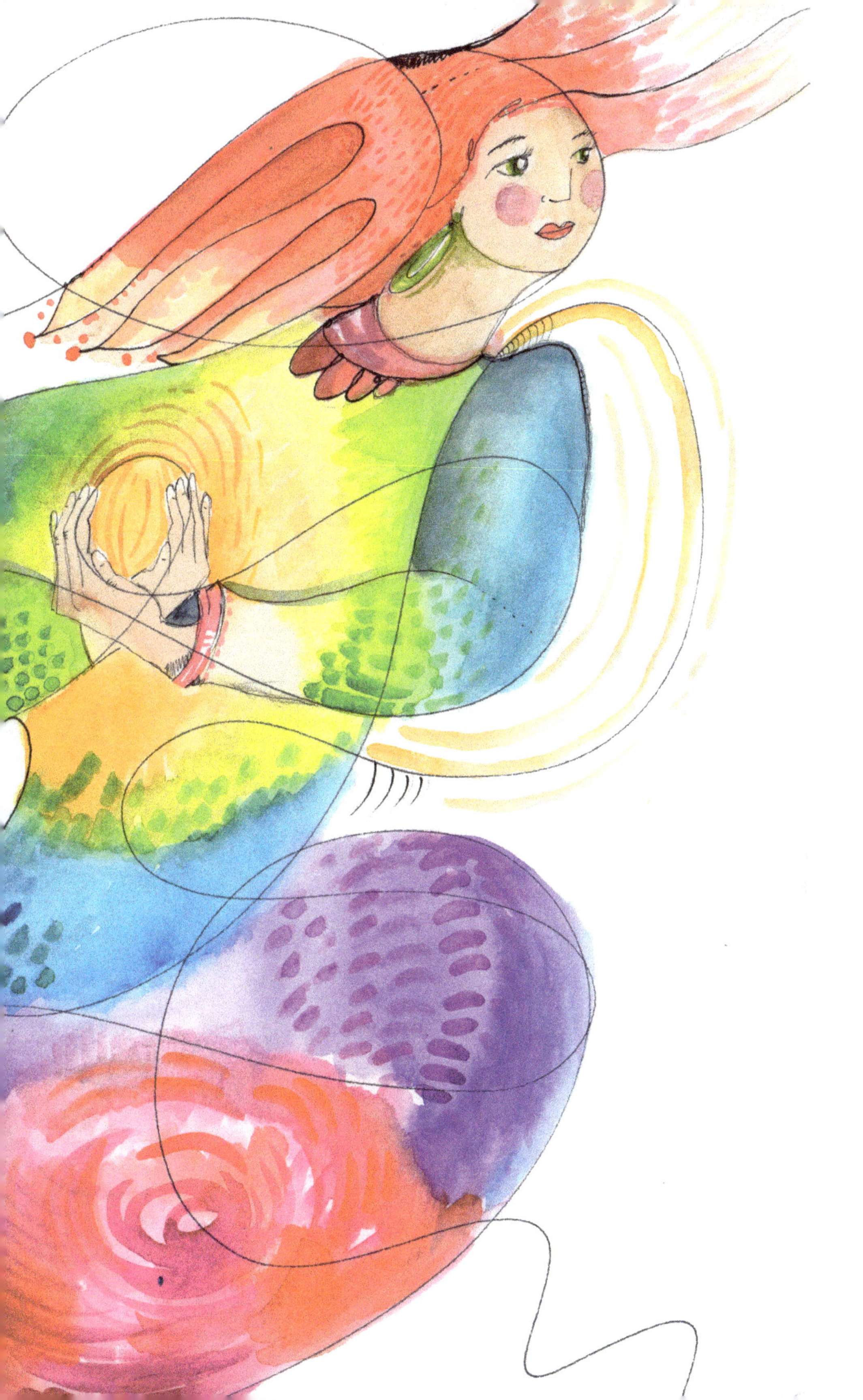

You know whom you remind me of?
Spirit –
how She can't be contained in one place,
but rather moves in and through all that is,
like the wind, blowing wherever
She pleases.

You who
patiently wait to play,
grateful for my attention,
willing to find nourishment
in crumbs of love,
not needing me to fall
on my knees, only to
show up and BE.

Again and again you
pass me the crystal ball
that reflects a mirror image of me,
an inspired woman longing
to find the soul food that feeds me
and share it with others.

Thank you, Imagination.

I'm ready
to receive
the reflection.

WONDER SEEKER

Hello, wonder seeker,
light keeper, day dreamer!
You are here. And, here I am, with you.
Funny how we keep meeting.
In this place. In that place.
Wherever you are, the quest carries on.
It's as if I've been following you.
Or are you trailing me?
Either way, we meet again.
I show up as the song of the sparrow
in the early morning hours
and the fireflies' glow in the dark of night.
I glisten in the forgotten cracks of sidewalks.

I honk playfully as a rubber squeaky toy.
Of course, you already get it.
You ARE a wonder seeker.
You and I are well acquainted.
Sometimes, though, you veer away from me.
But I'm vibrant and zesty.
I attempt to rouse you from your sleep.
Sometimes I'm shy.
Soft and sensitive.
I dim in the presence of gloom.
Yet, I'm here.
Waiting until we gather again.
And when we do, sparks fly.
You gasp with awe.
You gape open-mouthed, *Wow!*
You silently grin at my stealthy moves.
I am giddy.
Not everyone notices me.
But you do.
You ARE a wonder seeker.
So, today, when the doubt hedges in,
when the naysayers attempt to dampen your joy,
stay focused on me, okay?
Keep looking for me.
I promise I'll meet you there.
Wherever you are.
Whoever you are.
However you are.
I'll keep your hope aflame.
And, you.
You keep your heart open to goodness.

LANDING SPOT FOR IDEAS

There I was
folding my laundry,
in the quiet crevices
of a quite ordinary alcove,
when, WHOOSH —
She found me again.

She, a wonderfully whimsical idea,
looking for a place to land.

I can't tell you
where She came from,
only that I greeted her.
She landed on me gently,
like a cool drop of water
seemingly out of nowhere,
refreshing and surprising
all at once.

Soon enough, She
wrapped me with
ribbons of rainbows,
strange stirrings,
quirky questions,
intriguing imaginings.

She led me outdoors
to where the water lives
and motioned, *Don't be afraid.*
Dip your hands in. Your arms too! Yes!
Swim down, down to the bottom, to
see what you find.

The *what-ifs* creep in:
What-if I find something I'd rather not?
What-if the something I find leads to change?
What-if this change challenges the status quo?
What-if status quo resists who I am becoming?
What-if I fail at the whole thing?

MotherGod quietly observes me with love,
Her silent demeanor a strong support.
From within my core,
I feel (from the rumble in my belly)
failure is the only route to take.
Failure is the risk I must face.

Come with me now
and take the plunge;
a soaking-wet,
clumsy dive
toward mystery
at the heart of
a bottomless enigma.

LET US LIVE

There is nothing different
about this message
found better penned elsewhere
or by someone else.
But (maybe) at your next blink
this note will float to you at the ideal time
and the words will fall over you
like a healing balm.
You'll breathe in MotherGod
and find Her breath
moves to the tired places in your body
to refresh you
about the essence of living
that is yours to taste.

Here goes.

Let yourself live for today —
          a body of possibilities;
Let yourself listen to your favorite song —
          bass high, cruising down the road;
Let yourself dance, wherever you are —
          a solo performance for no one but yourself;
Let yourself speak to the living —
          with life-giving, love-opening words, a sweet breeze blowing.

Hello, bird! Fine morn, isn't it?
Oh, tree. You sure are a beauty. Thanks for blooming like you do.
Darling love. You are mine and I am yours. This is enough.

Let yourself skip the obligations and eat lobster on Saturday —
          practice the art of BEING.
Let yourself jump puddles after the rain —
          soaking wet, abuzz with laughter.
Let yourself applaud Spirit who lives in your BECOMING —
          an ongoing champagne celebration.

Tell me,
Why do you limit your living?
Why do you play it safe?
Why do you choose actions that look the same,
day after day, year after year,
lulling yourself into phantom motions
when your

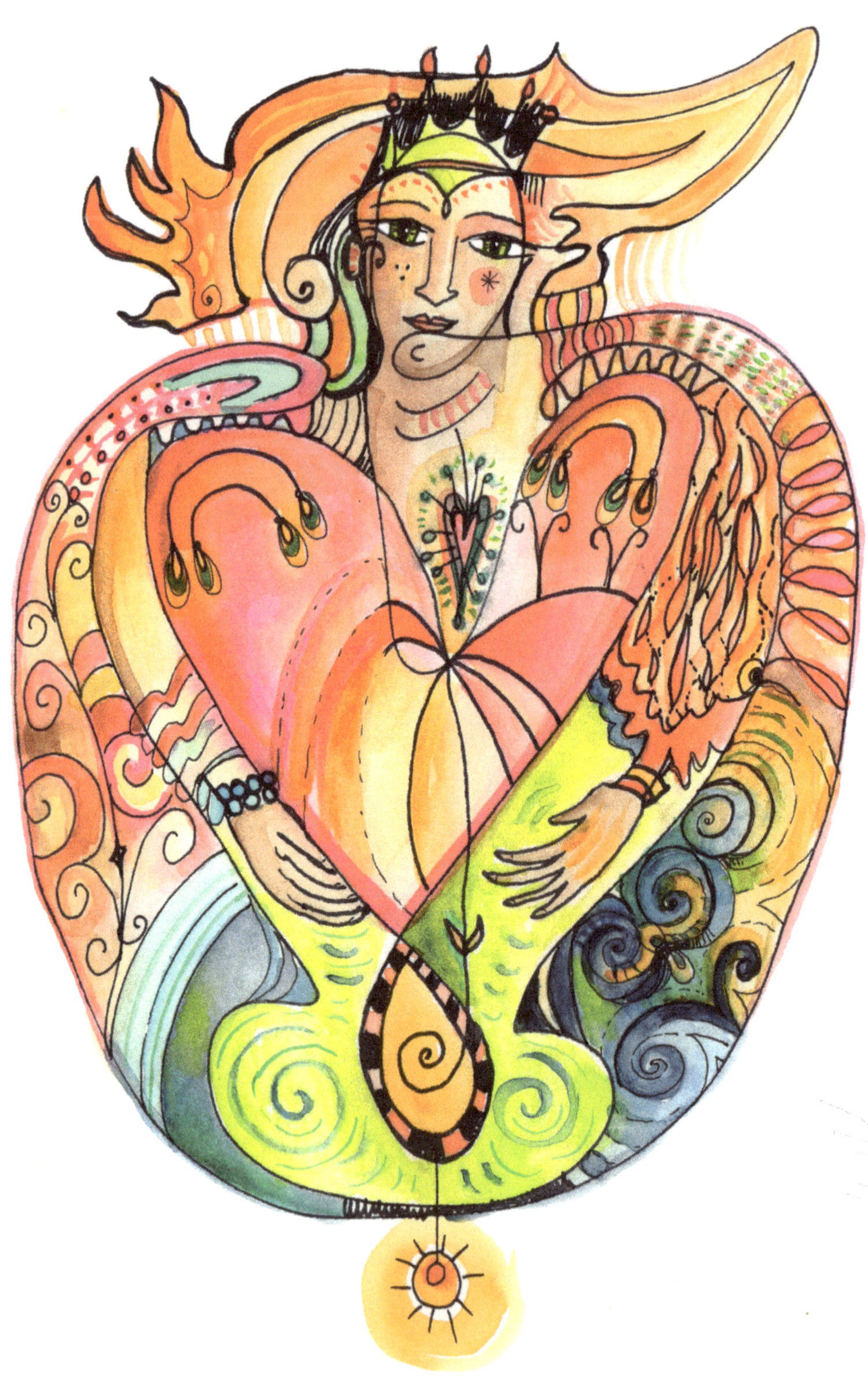

beating pulse
urges you to dance:
          listen for the dare,
          step out of line,
          risk your comfort,
urges you
to fully LIVE?

HOW TO KEEP A HOLY FIRE BURNING

Listen, first things first.
You must protect your flame
from the storm of naysayers.
This isn't selfish.
This is life or death to your Spirit.

In fact, I recommend you
place guardians around your ember.
These glee-givers will fan
your dancing flame.

When your flicker stirs,
you'll need space.
Lots of space to experiment
with marks of dawning.
This very act will release
a perfume of holy smoke.

Allow this regal aroma to
be swept by the open air
to draw those near
who long for
a restorative practice
to be with True Love.

Hear me when I say that
you also need containment.
A method to stay focused on
a what truly matters.
When you spread yourself thin,
it leads to a case of the grouchies.

Yes, yes — the awareness of environment
is imperative. You must keep alert:

an expansive wildfire can burst out on dry land,
just as saturated ground leads to a smothered smolder.

Another thing. I know you.

You still want to start checking boxes
from the list of *What I Should Be Doing*.
No boxes. No shoulds.
Trust me, you'll go to sleep and burn out.
Best to keep with the natural cadence
that gleams through you.

Once you've learned from
the ebb and flow of your inner fire
and your blaze is a bountiful bouquet,
take care to tend to it often.

When you stay present to the Now
your inside ears will begin to open to
what your fertile fire needs.
For those who have ears to hear…

Stay awake.

Keep creating.

Take a risk.

Rest when rest calls.

Finally, remember
who designed
your disco dazzle
in the first place.

SHINE

The pain is swept into the corner
with cobwebs and day-old crumbs.
I attempt to dismiss the tired remains
until my bare feet step on it,
the discomfort palpable.

I focus on the dis-ease,
missing my sliver of soul glimmer,
a slice of personal sparkle
mixed into the grime,
clouded from eyesight.
Seems, as I tidy up the exterior,
the ache of my heart amplifies,
Dampens my inner flame
to a cooling ember.

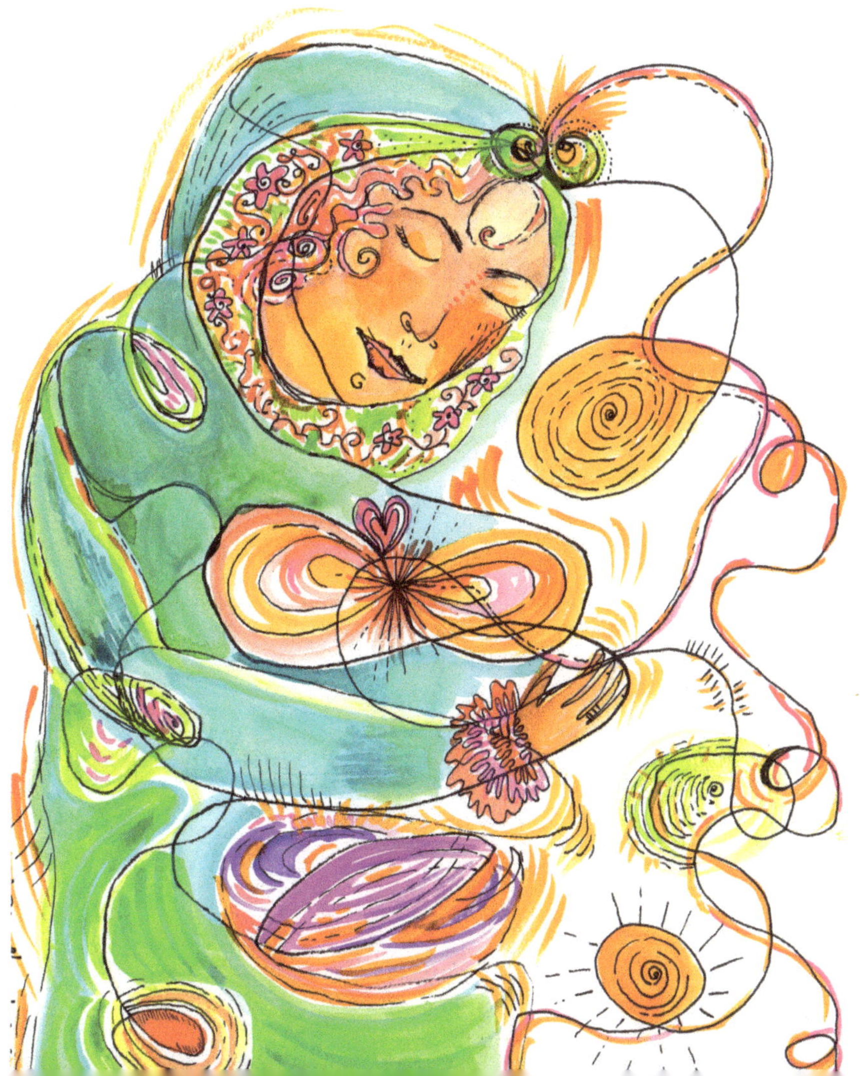

I view it in you, too.
How your sheen
has been polished carefully,
preened into politeness,
the press of life a toll-taker.
Yet, as we share a cookie,
your eyes tell a different story:
one of silly whims and
wacky tales, and laughter
spills over from your
crystal-laden caverns, your
fiery kindle aglow.

I realize,
you, too,
are unaware
of your secret flame.

How can it be that
we shield ourselves
from our innate luminosity,
a grace-given gift?

Why do we cleanse
the very thing that makes
our heart beat while we
dwell on the dust?

I wait for your eyes to open
and take in what I recognize in you:
your beautiful curiosity,
your refined listening,
your heart-centered hub.

Maybe I'll find you
waiting for me too.

How do we support
one another to
boldly declare our divinity
with no apology needed?

Together, we wait.
We share our lives.
We champion one another's expansion.
I inspire your voice; you inspire mine.
And.

We wait.
To believe it for ourselves.
To believe we deserve
the grace-filled pizazz
already within us.

While you wait,
let this soak in:
Yes.
You are majestic.
Yes.
Playful pomp is yours to have,
especially alongside grief.

And if you aren't able to claim this,
it's okay.
Because I affirm it for you
as you will for me.

Side by side,
we help each other
keep the flame aglow.
We are forever bound
in love.

OPEN TO POSSIBILITY

Look at your toes.
They are there
to take you through
the unlocked door, the silent
threshold that urges
you to embrace the mist of
childlike awe.

Do you notice
how the hawk
glides through
the blue expanse,
keen to her senses,
swoops down to
grab her feast,
trusts she will find
what she needs?

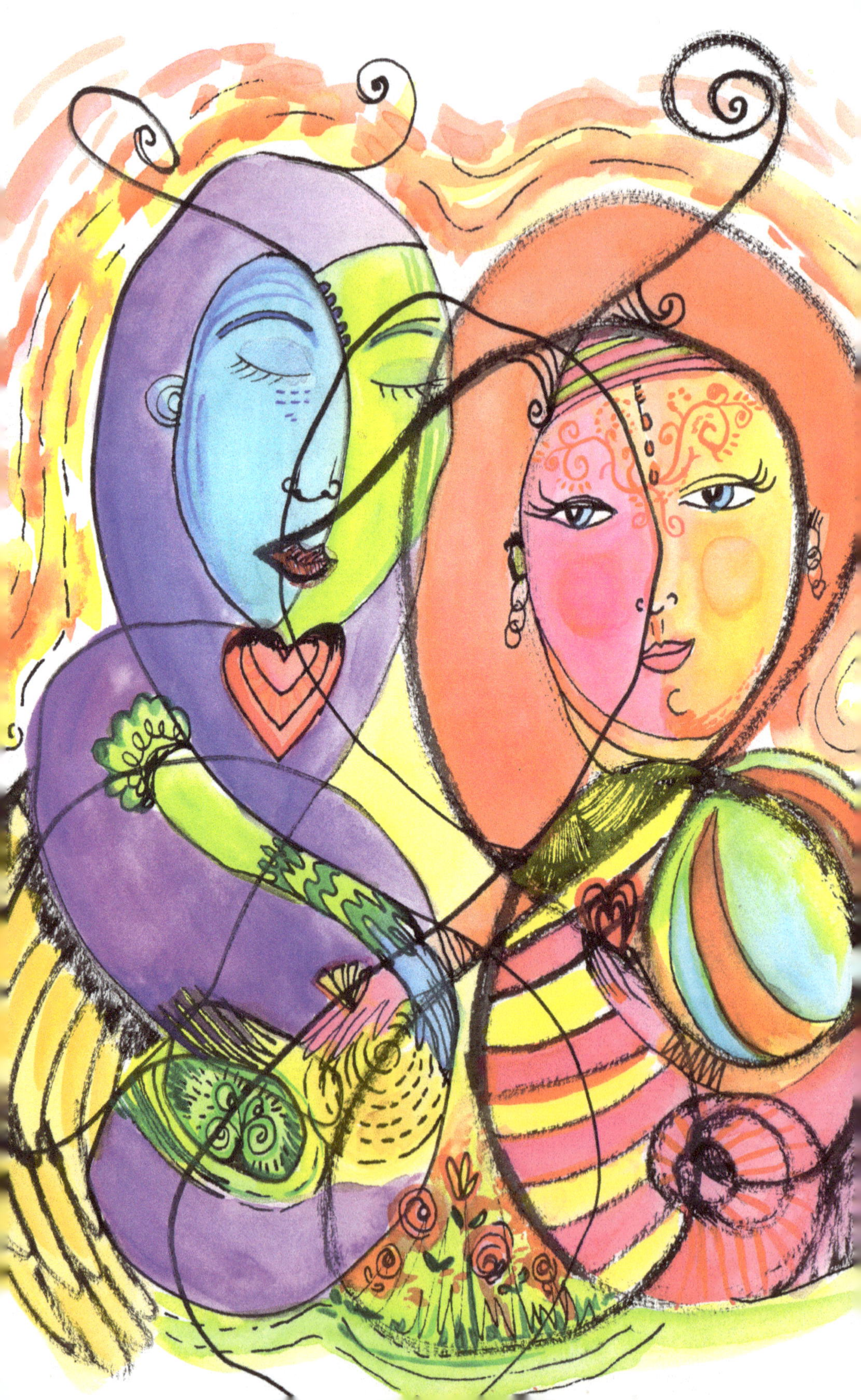

What about you?
Do you doubt your senses?

(Why?)
You too, have intuition,
a knowing
that guides your
inward star.
Lean in, listen.
Touch the luster
of your diamond.
As your finger trembles
to point to reverent truth,
don't be blinded when
beams of gold
pour upon you.

Instead,
open yourself to imagination —
this gold is for you,
a shimmer that glistens
upon your crown,
and moves
into the starlit dusk
around you;
this is the gold of
dream-raking
womb-baking
heart-waking.

Why limit yourself
to human goals
when you can soar
on blessed wind,
unleash the
sacred unknown —
a chance
to gather sparkles
and throw them
beyond the edges
of your making.

PLAY WITH ME

If I could display the answers you want,
I'd lay them with care on a tray for your consumption.

All I can offer is a yellow brick road,
a winding way that leads you to the home of your heart.

I cannot tell you the secrets of the images I conceive,
where they come from or what they are; I barely comprehend this myself.

What I do know is that the practice of showing up to presence
opens the gate for loving, ethereal energies to work on my behalf.

They come to
shine the moon,
offer guidance,
pour liquid gold
into my glittering chalice.

They come to unlock the door of possibility.

Here I am —
swimming,
praising,
guzzling
this stream of love.

Her pure nature restores me entirely
Listen — I long for you to drink from her waters.

Come, have a taste. Play with me!
Let's paint in the moonlight together!

You'll see —
the portal of inspiration is HERE
for both of us.

IN THE BEGINNING

In the beginning,
Poet created beauty and love.
There was no form yet to be seen,
the void was the womb of creation.

When the contractions of Wisdom began,
the waters stirred and
Poet spoke the first Word:

Let there be light.

And the light revealed
treasure within the oblivion.

And the light within all was good.
And there was sleeping. And there was waking — the first day.
 And Poet listened for Wisdom
and wrote Words of a haiku:

Let there be an arch
to pull apart the waters —
Clear blue sky, emerge!

And there was sleeping. And there was waking — the second day.

Poet was a harvester
who wrapped arms wide around dusty earth
and spoke, *I love you, land!*

And, Poet was a gatherer
who attracted particles of water
and purred, *I love you, seas!*

Then Poet's warm breath went
into the marrow of the land —
a devotion to flourish
rose from within the soil.

Fresh green joy sprouted forth.
Plant joy. Tree joy. Fruit joy.
These seeds of joy spread.

Poet saw that it was good.
And there was sleeping. And there was waking — the third day.
Poet looked up at the sky arch.
Poet tuned to Wisdom, hummed a Word —

Let there be orbs of radiance
that light the earth.
Let their presence be a reminder
of rhythm, a sign that brings
steady ritual to the living —
each day, each season, each year.

Poet threw stars into the arch.
They winked at Poet. Poet winked back.

Poet saw that it was good.
And there was sleeping. And there was waking — the fourth day.

Poet wasn't done. More notions needed to become matter.
Poet said,
Let there be gills that provide air,
long tentacles that squirm,
mama turtles that stand
for pilgrimage.
Let there be wings that fly,
beaks that squawk,
dove pigeons that stand
for peace.

And Poet saw that it was good.

Poet blessed the water-beings
and bird-beings with Wisdom and Word,
I give you the potential to create.
Go, bring more water-beings into the world.
Go, build your nests and nurture your eggs.
Let the mystery increase in beauty.

And there was sleeping. And there was waking — the fifth day.

Poet looked to the land and envisioned the empty fields
filled with hairy beasts.

Poet shouted,
Come, come, you wild animals!
Swing from the trees, prowl in your pack, roar your roar
Come, come, you working animals.
Eat some grass, lay your eggs, baaa your baaa
Come, come, you ground dwellers;
slither to the left, crawl to the right, croak your croak.
And Poet saw that it was good.

Then Poet conferred with Wisdom and Word and said,
Let us make beings in our image,

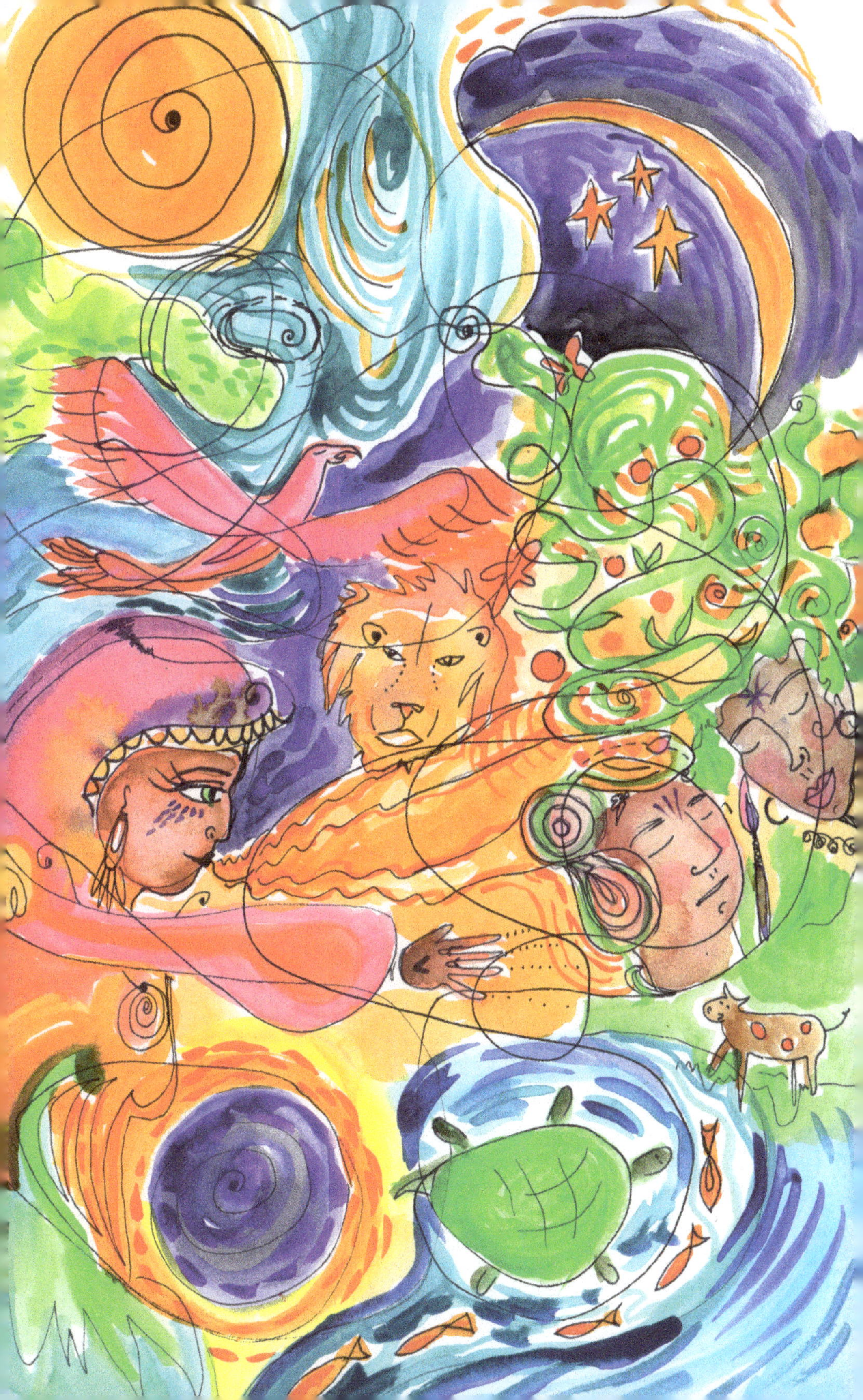

so they may care for all we've created.
So Poet grabbed hands with Wisdom and Word
and frolicked in a circle. They laughed at the inkling.
They all took a lively inhalation
and blew sacred air upon the ground.
The dust rose up and became human figures,
Artist and Muse.

Poet blessed them and said,
I give you the capacity to innovate freely.
Go, bring more of you onto the earth.
Let the intricacy of your BE-ing increase.
I give you the power of love
over all of creation.
This power is meant for you to witness
the bird-beings in the air,
the water-beings in the seas,
the creatures on land,
and to do so with affection.

I am the great Giver.
I give everything I've created for you to share!
Here! Take it! You are part of ALL THIS!
I hand you
the plant joy, the tree joy, the fruit joy!

It's meant to eat
so that you take joy in regularly.
Share this joy with the animals.
Let them take in joy with you.
Be considerate of all the living.

And it was so.

Poet, Wisdom and Word saw all they had created,
and it was very good.

And there was sleeping. And there was waking — the sixth day.

Thus, beauty and love were completed in all their vast array.

On the seventh day, all the creations of Poet were present.
Poet took a seat on green grass joy next to yellow Dog.
Poet rested. Poet delighted. Poet played.
Poet named this day *holy* because stillness
allowed Poet to revel in what had been made.

And it was. Good.

DANGER WORD

Wily, this word that rolls — *should*.

>Dangles and stretches, the
purple wisteria of words,
an alluring, empty promise,
a choking vine.

Should.

>Winds through
daily bread,
through your middle,
into consciousness.

Should.

>Spoken from within,
a haunted internal arising —
(I should) do better, be stronger,
go farther, move faster.

Should.

>Spoken from others,
a shot toward your tenderness.
Your lack becomes their headline,
your fumbles their top story.

Should.

>Tossed from your throat
a cheap shot toward someone else,
about their one precious life,
their soulful decisions.

Today —

>you and I waken to
the tendency that *should*
holds us (and others) down.

Today —

>you reach your hands to release
should to Poet who reforms.
you push your feet into the ground
and stand firm in who you are.

Today —

>the organic bell of love resounds.
You are received as you are.
You receive others as they come.

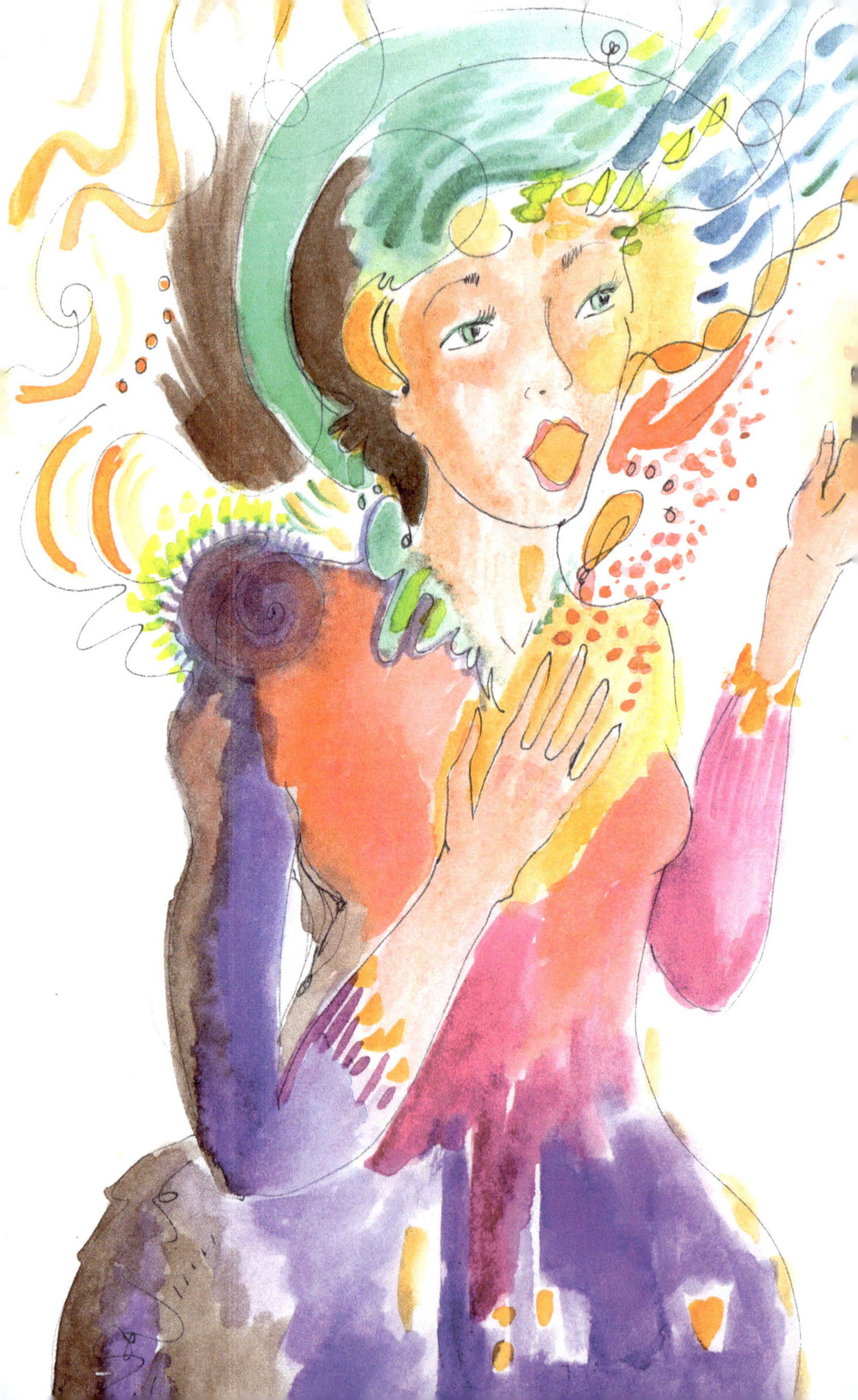

SPEAK YOUR VOICE

You haven't taken a vow of silence.
But you've deemed there are certain things
better left unsaid.

When you've tried to
champion the cause,
speak the alternate view,
you've been met with resistance,
or worse,
isolation.

You don't want to ruffle
too many feathers, take a chance
on not pleasing the listener.
It's only natural that
you've wrapped your bruised voice
in burlap and steel wire. You stick to
pallid pleasantries. But –
take notice.
This is no time to remain silent.

Those "certain things" you've deemed are better
left unsaid are the very words you need. The utterance
of healing, hope, consideration.

You don't need
more anger spewed,
more complaint,
more hate passed along.

You are the powerful one
whose words are delicately linked
to vulnerability. You are the one
who values Mother of Mercy.

Do you hear the reflection of your Spirit?

Your words are wishing to have wings.
They fancy taking flight.
Who are you to keep them tucked down?

I sense your trepidation.
> *I don't want to offend.*
> *Who needs my opinion anyway?*

Can you trust that your experiences
have given you a vantage point that matters?

A view that needs to be expressed?

When a voice is kept locked up,
words tend to grow a dense, mossy film
and are vented as cynicism
from a wounded place.

If you are stuck in this place,
here's what to do:

First, remember —
you are linked to Love. Then,
string your opinion
through the eye of a sacred needle;
sew it through your heart
where wings await. Then,
stitch each word to a feather of air
and allow them to flutter
through your voice box.

If you and I speak our truth
grounded in love,
whom shall we fear?
That we will be disliked,
spat upon, knocked over?

Maybe.

But by staying silent
we are the ones who put
ourselves on hot coals, muffle
our utterance of affection to
a lost world.

Can we? Voice brave?
Can we? Bring heart?

Yes. We can.

We must.

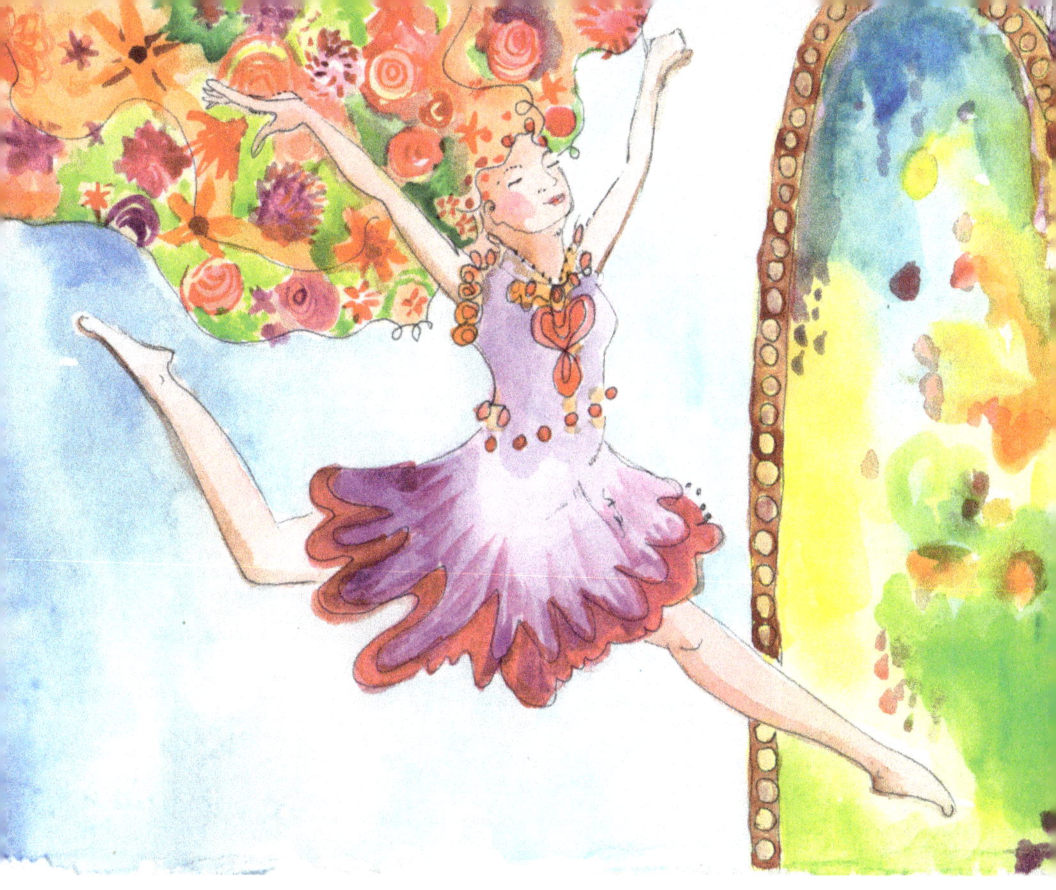

CHASE YOUR DREAM

I hear your song—
the lyrics longing to be known,
a rhythmic pulse of blood and tears
to prove what you are made of,
a common dream of worth.
I look in your eyes—
it's as if I'm staring in a mirror
with you on the other side.
I want to protect you
and embrace you all at once.
I understand your passion—
who am I to dampen your flame?
I still have dreams I'm chasing,
senseless though they may seem to those
who've by now snuffed their own flame out.
This is what I need to say to you:

Go, chase your dream.
Run through the brisk wind.
Take a chance,
fall down and cry hard,
taste your food.
Learn from those wiser than yourself. And yes,
set out on the road less traveled (you know,
the one that has made all the difference).
As your legs lead you to
catch lightning bugs and
blaze after stars, remember this:
You do not have to prove yourself.
You are (already) intimately known
by the Loving Poet who longs for you.
You are good. In fact, very good. You are wanted.
Not for what you do. Not for what you produce.
Not for the success you gain.
Not for who you'll become.
No, but for who you already are. In this moment.
YOU are made in the image
of creative Love.
L
(listen, listen.)
This is the truth
that makes all the difference.

Receive the love.
Share your shine.

THERE YOU GO

A quiet launch,
bread rises with no fanfare;

a summer silence,
petal leaf opens to the luster of the moon;

a first flight,
baby bird-wings span to trust the air.

Sandwiched in the middle of
riots and illness,
anger and death,

a door appears.
Opportunity greets you.

The hidden Holy trails beside you,
a visible sign emerges before you.

You trace the thread of the heart
and watch plans come to fruition.

There is no one there to notice.
No balloons rise.
No congratulations are spoken.
No pat on the back.

It's a silent reckoning,
a nod to yourself —
you are doing the work
of your heartstrings.

You smoke sage,
sway your arms with the wind,
smile to Earth Mama below your feet;
take the oil,
anoint your body with care.

Initiate yourself as
the gentle artist you are,
as spiritual midwife,
feminine mystic,
teacher of empathy,
rainbow mother,
story poet,
circle guide,
soul kindler.

In this process —
you become yourself.
A person who claims your value
which cannot be erased.

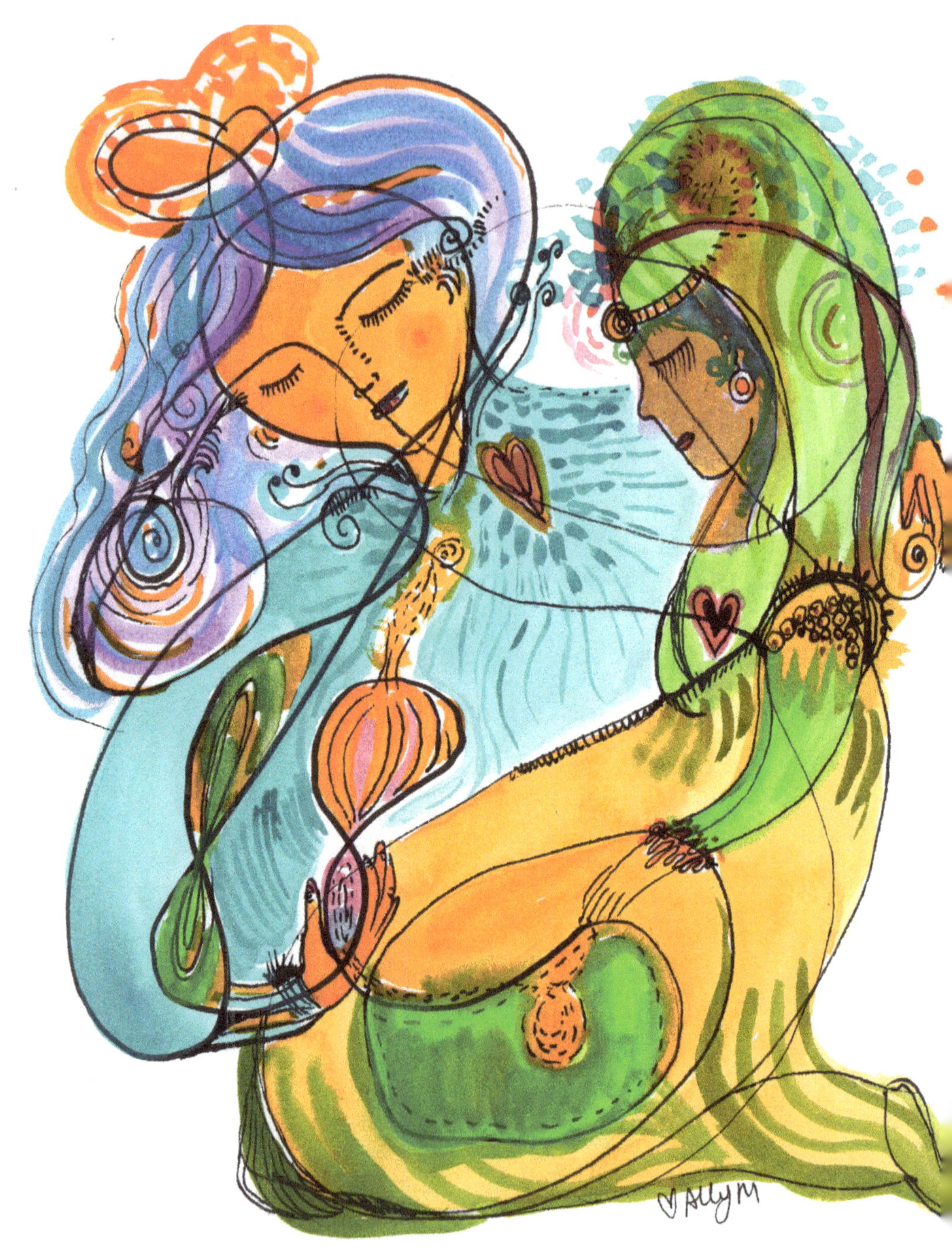

A POETIC REFLECTION ON *I AM WONDER*

Maybe it took a moment
to stir the crystal gems of your memory,
but it's been there all along, hasn't it?

The buzz, buzz of your imaginings,
the sing-song hum in your heart.
It feels good to acknowledge
what you've known all along,
doesn't it?

You ARE a WONDER-filled being
with marvelous ideas. Boom.
Why not explore this on the page?

Go ahead and draw a simple heart shape.
Ask for an idea as you begin to color your heart.
Listen in. What do you hear?

Write your dreamy idea in the center of your heart.
Now, let it fizz and pop
with circles and stars, dots and bursts.
Add a rainbow of color;
move your idea outward
from the core of your heart.

Take this bubbling possibility to the edges.

Where does it go?
Whom does it greet?
What goodness do you feel in your body?

Now, give your heart wings
and watch it lift you into flight.

Yes. You hold a boundless amount
of sacred goodness within yourself.

Let it go.

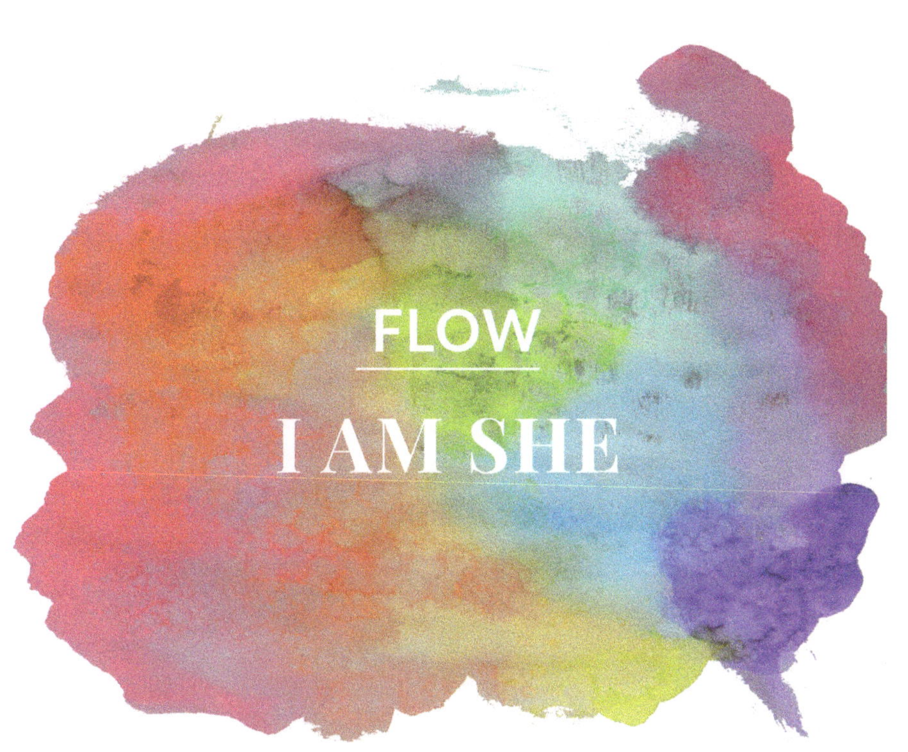

*Poems to Swim in the
Mother's Love*

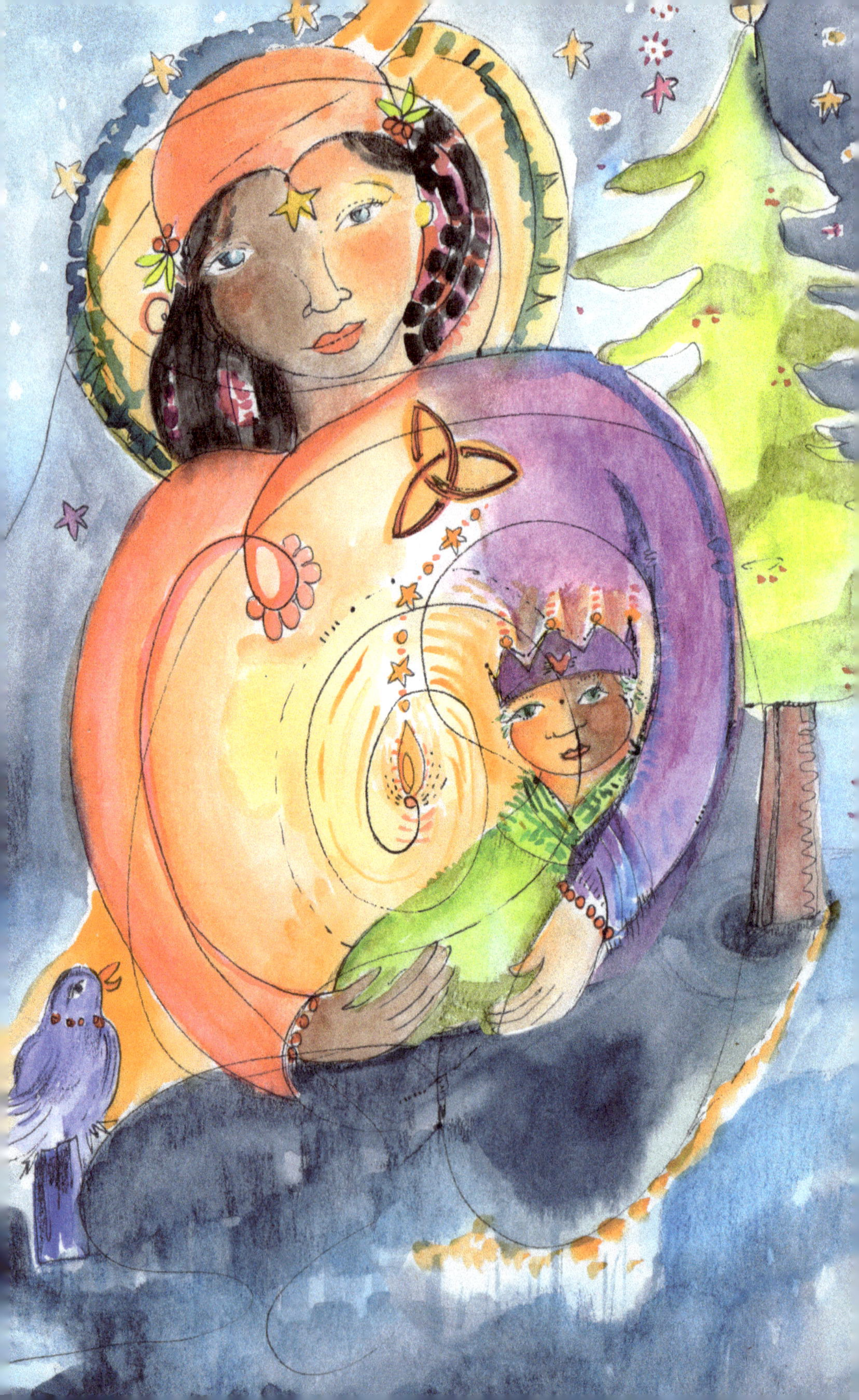

THE MOTHER JOURNEY

The earnest quality is hard to resist —
the bright shine, the graphic glow,
the gleam of adventure
ready to burst from within.

Your innocence drips charm
toward those who want to sculpt you anew.

Yet the purity you carry is not naivety,
nor is it ignorance of the systems of the world.

Trust me, your nature
leads you to sniff like a wolf,
to hunt with the eyes of a hawk,
and spin clever concepts in the night.

The road travels hard,
your blood pulses steadily
as energy vibrates within.

The trek takes you deeper, darker —
into the resources of yourself. Sleeping,
shadows bundle you in blessed warmth
as crevices of light make their way into your dreams.
Waking, you cradle the ache and awe together,
embrace the twins of your heart.

Your womb's heartbeat finds nourishment
in the mystic regions of mother-cave.

Ripened wings move through the birth canal
to their expansion of flight.

Your spellbinding quality leads some to resist
your high vibration,
your auric heat,
your esoteric insight.

Still,

You become the mother of your children.

You become the mother of all children.

You become the mother of yourself.

Still,
You send the dove of peace to fly through the world.

This, the mother journey—
an invitation for all
to let the night mold you (once more)
and the glint of dawn lead.

FIERCE MAMA

No meek and mild lady,
no pasty, polite socialite —
this one,
a woman after MotherGod's own heart,
brave virgin girl,
clips the string of expectations,
snips the cord of cultural norms,
carves space in her feminine bowl —
falls into a wide open *Yes* and
stretches into wily woman.
She enters into a friendship embrace, goes to
the one who supports her in tender ripening.
Together, wombs leap, energy flows.
Now, this one, fire in her belly,
glorifies the Holy One amid trial,
stands tall for justice.
She moves to the song of mercy,
the prayer of her lineage.
This one, fierce mama,
births brilliance in open air,
a span of dirt and crumbs.
She and her beloved are
a mysterious spectacle of kinship.
Wise woman
ponders in untouchable spaces.
Blessed Mother
holds a shield of light,
a child of hope,
prays you and I
nurse this
infant of grace
we carry within.

TO BE CARRIED

Why am I surprised?
Isn't this how I've heard
the Star of the Sea loves?

When I
loosen the grip of logic
and look for the spaciousness of love,
there I am,
carried.

Carried, I ride on the wind.
Effortless, I am a bird,
wings open, alive with
the lift of air beneath me.

Carried, I swim with the stream.
Untethered, I am a fish
flexing fin, floating with
the rush of sea around me.

When I
table-talk with resistance,
curious to opposition,
there I am,
held.

Held, I drop into secure sleep
in the arms of protection.
Eyes closed peacefully, I trust
the One who embraces me.

Held, I press my soft belly
into sweet, wordless wonder.
Visions appear, and I cherish
the presence of patterns just for me.

When I
waken to broad belonging,
accept the obscure,
there I am,
connected.

Connected, I raise my elation
to the love revelation.
Hands open, I receive

abundance that is enough
for you and me.

Connected, my classic pearls
come undone; tradition loosened.
Pearls of wisdom prompt me —
to go, be free, be me.

Met where I am,
this is how Spirit loves —
She carries,
She holds,
She connects.

YOUR POWER

Your power returned to you the day
you chose to place the stapler down
from the boxy bulletin board,
to move beyond the confines where
your creative savvy flies free.

Your power returned to you the day
you resigned from beating yourself up
for "brokenness," blaming yourself
for all you "aren't" —
to embrace the abundant goodness
and sheer beauty of all you are.

Your power returned to you the day
you laid down the ingrained pattern
of serving everyone before yourself in order
to foster yourself first, which led
to a natural outflow of personal passion.

Your power returned to you the day
you dropped the belief
that you don't belong and
took your place as one who
holds significance.

Your power returned to you the day
you found decorating your home
wasn't a frivolous hobby, but

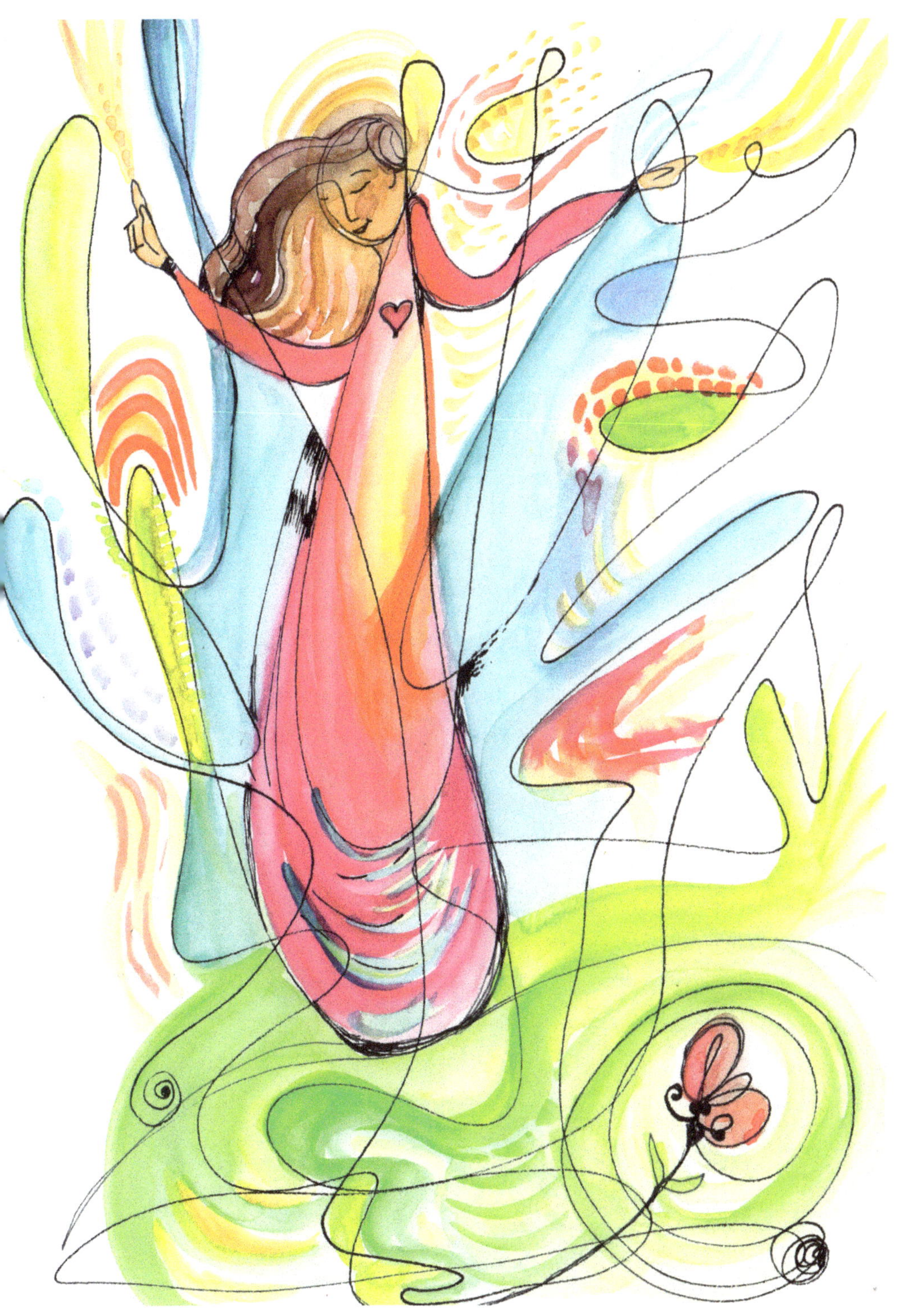

rather a recipe of hospitality to
invite people into rest and renewal.

Your power returned to you the day
you quit judging other women
to make yourself feel better, and
took up the torch of compassion
and celebration for your sisters.

Your power returned to you the day
you turned off the TV,
left the screens behind,
and went outside to put your toes
in the grass, ears open to birdsong,
and said *Hello!* to Mother Earth.

Your power returned to you the day
you grasped your
love of green gardening
was a trusty medicine
conveyed by your ancestors.

Your power returned to you the day
you ended cycles of extensive education
to be regarded as "equal" to your male peers
and instead claimed yourself "enough" as you are
to birth your place in the world.

Your power returned to you the day
you dropped the weight of
carrying the whole burden
so you could hone in on your own life
and do it with fierce generosity.

Your power returned to you the day
you tasted your acidic shadows
and, instead of rejecting them,
chose to usher them
into the heart of your story.

Your power returned to you the day
you unearthed nuggets of gold
from your years around the sun,
cleansed the mire and muck from them
to listen to your own wisdom.

Your power returned to you the day
you claimed your passion as Medicine Woman,
an integral offering to society,
and crossed over the threshold
to bring healing to others.

Your power returned to you the day
you reviewed your shopping habits
and realized the amazing ability you had
at your fingertips to change the economy
by where and how you choose to spend.

Your power returned to you the day
you ended silencing yourself
to keep others comfortable
and opted to speak out
about the injustices you see.

Your power returned to you the day
you recognized the impact your words,
art, and actions have in this world.
You heard the hum of legacy, urging,
What will I leave for the next generation?

Your power returned to you
the day you left the Table of Approval
for the Feast of Grace —
where you chose to celebrate your dynamic Spirit,
In all your brilliant becoming.

WEAVER OF THE THREAD

The ancient women sat together,
a stitch of red thread through
the sacred temple veil,
a weave of mythic tales
whispered to one another.

A song chanted:

Pass the thread, pass the thread;
Ooooo, la la.
Come together, come together;
Ooooo, la la.

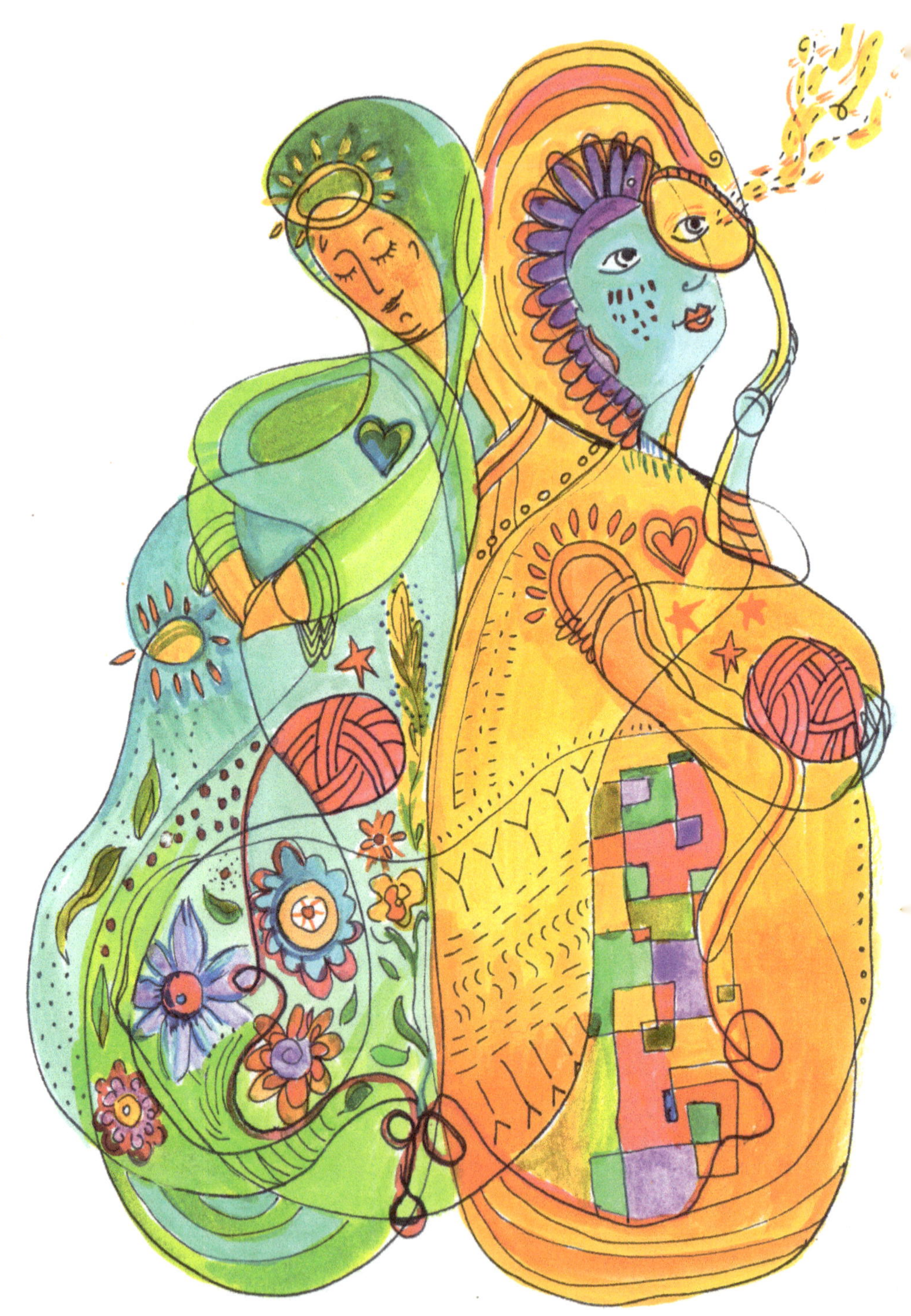

Claim your voice, claim your voice.
Give the blessing, Give the blessing.
Ooooo, la la.

Passed into the hands of ladies,
slow love sewn into quilts
to warm small children,
a lace of laughter through
each fiber.

Pass the thread, pass the thread.
Ooooo, la la.

Slid into wrinkled hands
of the feminine, maker of flags
for the love of her nation,
a prayer of peace
blessed into the future wave.

Pass the thread, pass the thread.
Ooooo, la la.

Received into my mother's needle,
crafted into small x's,
a masterpiece of embroidery,
her care deliberately sewn
into each winter's stitch.

Pass the thread, pass the thread.
Ooooo, la la.

I'm handed the red thread
in the bowl of my palm;
I wrap it around my slender wrist,
a visible reformer, sparkles with
transformative love.

Pass the thread, pass the thread.
Ooooo, la la.

I hand the skein to my sister,
she and I forever wed
by a cord of blood;
we eye each other with care,
companions not competitors.

Passed around the circle,
a mixed bag of pilgrims
shoulder to shoulder, their
trepidation dissolves to reveal
a witness of belonging.

The thread cannot be contained,
thrown out to community
where leaders thirst for meaning,
a tool that reveals their truth,
I'm overextended. I long for the trees.

This crimson is woven
through states and countries, an
undetected fiber where people
lead sacred formation in
ordinary settings.

Do you see? This scarlet cord
falls from the window and
wraps the wide world
(the full spectrum)
in a raw love of reception.

This thread is a
channel and holder
of all stories, a symbol of
timeless direction
for the masses.

Still, here and now,
the ancient women sit together,
they spin, cackle
and chant their song. Listen!

Pass the thread, pass the thread.
Ooooo, la la.
Come together, come together.
Ooooo, la la.
Claim your voice, claim your voice.
Give the blessing, Give the blessing.
Ooooo, la la.

I am a weaver of the thread.
A claimer of the good.
A sharer of the story.

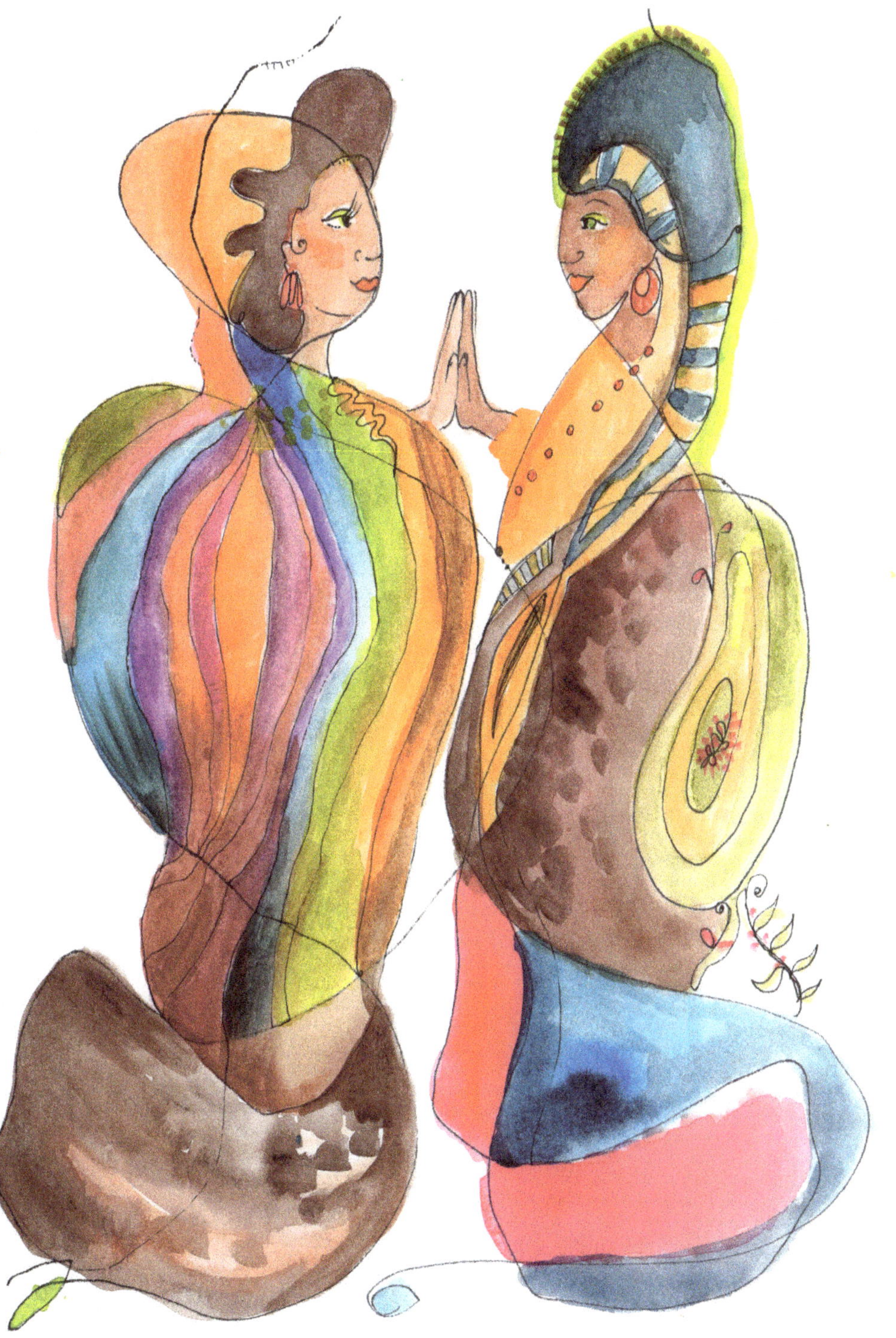

Here — I pass it to you.
Tell me,
*will you receive it
and pass it on?*

AS YOURSELF

Today, you hear it said,
Love your neighbor as yourself.

*(as yourself)
(as yourself)*

This echo resonates in your core.
You never heard it this way.
It was usually:
Love God. Love others. The end.

*(as yourself)
(as yourself)*

There it is again.
A bell rings deep within.

*If I'm to love my neighbors as myself,
how DO I love myself?*, you ponder.

Your non-stop rush of hustle-bustle comes to mind:

Quick eating. Limited exercise. Doing for others.
Crumbs left over for yourself.

You catch a snippet of harsh self-criticism in your mind;
a thought you'd never dare say to another. Hmph.

*(as yourself)
(as yourself)*

This is no mundane moment.
Today, you decide to rewrite your story
and practice loving yourself.

You begin by watering
the organic ground of your being.
(where Wisdom resides)

You tune in to your natural foresight
and affirm what you hear.

(still, small voice)

You root a rainbow arc in your heart
and affirm your significance.

(garden of your soul)

You support your seedlings instead of
sapping up the suggestions of others.

(the Wisdom path)

You rest even though
rest isn't popular.

(Sabbath activism)

You say, *No,* even though
speaking *No* ruffles feathers.

(cultural resistance)

As you show up again and again,
you learn soul care.

This is *no* ordinary day.

Today, you don Sophia's flame upon your crown
and write a love story of YOU.

And in loving yourself,
you pour out your offering

from a grounded and healthier place.

And THAT
is something to CELEBRATE.

FOR SUCH A TIME AS THIS

Walk, don't run, little girl.
>   *But, I was made to run free!*

Color inside the lines, little girl.
>   *But, I'm created to color with my imagination!*

Dress like a lady, little girl.
>   *But, aren't I more than the clothes I wear?*

Here's your make-up, young lady.
>   *But, why do I need to cover myself?*

Hush, young lady.
>   *But I have something important to say.*

This is the way it is, young lady.
>   *But I view it differently.*

Why aren't you married, young woman?
>   *Does my worth come from a romantic relationship?*

When will you have babies, young woman?
>   *Am I only what I produce?*

You aren't made to lead, woman.
>   *Why are my gifts diminished?*

Woman, your voice is a disturbance.
>   *For such a time as this for my voice to rise.*

MR. ROYALTY

Hello
Mr. Royalty,
Your Highness,
Sir —

All due respect, but
I need to tell you,
I've tried your strategic method —
for decades.
Spoken words (you) approved (me) to repeat,

Knees grounded, metered and measured,
nodded to all the stories you told. Oh yes,

I colored within the lines with precision,
kept my doodles black and white,
my curious voice a silent coffin.

Mr. Royalty,
You learned early on
that when a woman speaks
with her resonance of truth,
her voice reverberates
at the highest level of kinship
with all the living.

You grasped her impact.
You were smart.
You used your magnetism to shift and shape,

WHOOSH — life-giving art of Madonna and child replaced,
ZAP — pivotal stature of Magdalene stripped,
POOF — women vanished from the pulpit; male priests given full power.

The crazy thing is: your trickery worked:

you convinced me
— I'm better behind you than beside you,
— the creative worth I bring is merely a hobby,
— to trust only the senses that make "sense."

Am I dangerous? Maybe.
Do you fear the power I have that you don't?

Hmmm…
Your Highness, truthfully,
my intuition tells me:
Your technique isn't working anymore.
It's falling flat.

I know, I know,
your promises of greatness are alluring,
the walls you build seem safe,
but your rehearsed lines lack Spirit flow
and your bravado is plain old silly.
You and I both know this.
Don't we? *(Ahem.)*

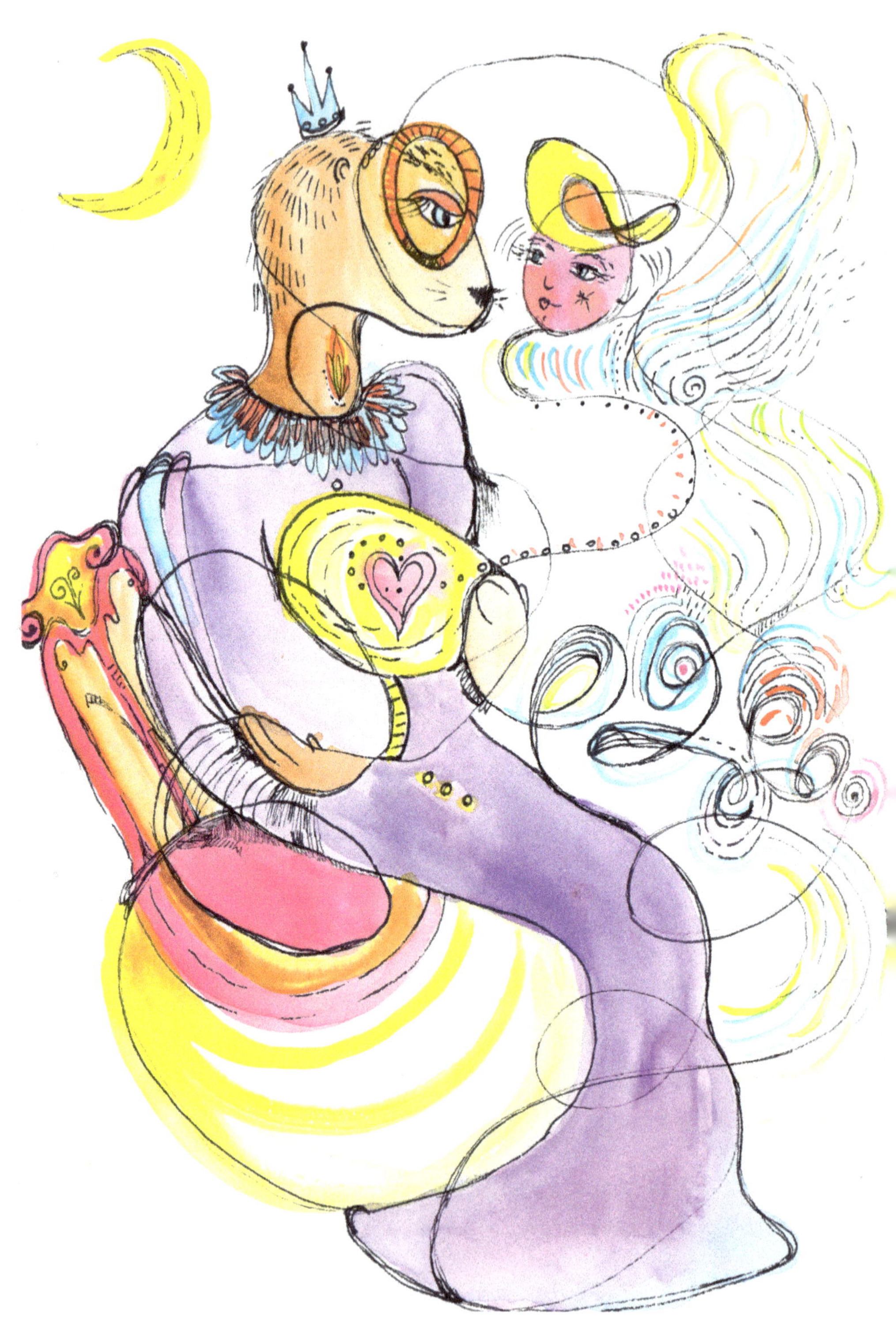

I mean, why the magnification?
Exaggeration is nothing more than
a cover-up of your fear.
I think you may be scared.

Mr. Royalty,
it's okay.
We've all been there.
Let's pause, shall we?

(deep breath)

I have to ask you this:
*Are you interested in learning
secrets beyond the constitution of man?*

I'm willing to teach you.
But, you need to lessen your resistance.
This will be hard.
For so long you've insisted
you possessed the "right" way.
Listen, it's time to admit —
your "way" has exhausted masses
and exploited resources.
Why not cease stirring your toxic potion
and feast at my table for a while?

If you say, *Yes,*
the door of foresight opens

like Joseph —
you may open to messages of angels
and stand by those who are cast out

like the Magi —
you may dream to travel a different route
and you will boldly go

like Christ —
you may welcome women to work at your side
and co-create a world tapped with liminal messages.

This narrow gate is an opportunity
to embrace palpable love that lies in your lap,
to extol the felt wind that touches your skin,
to trust failure as an opening
to a Love-source larger than you.

Are you ready
to move past the fifth sense?

I'm ready to take you there.
Come, if you dare, and
sit at the feet of feminine intuition.

THE DIVINE FATHER LET ME GO

The Father let me go.
He said, *It's time you find your way.*

    I don't want to leave this safety net. This is all I've known.

The Son speaks, *There's another path. An organic way of listening. Go.*

    I don't want to go. In this place, I know the rules.
    I know what is expected of me. I know what prayers to speak.

Another voice rises; Her tone is grace, *This is not your place any longer.*
    Come with me.
I —
argue with all my might;
blame with all my spite;
fret with all my fright;
Then, a speck of light.
This glow isn't a simple ray of gentle ease;
this glare urges me
to unravel everything I think I know about the King of Kings.
This beacon points to the difficult,
has me on my knees inspecting
the disappearance of Lilith,
the intuition of Rahab,
the truth about snakes.
My eyes open to the systemic toxicity
of the ground I stand upon.
I mourn the twisted history I've been given.
No, this lemon aroma isn't all bright beam.
It cleans out the clutter in my soul.
Here,
I'm advised to bow to what culture considers strange:
dreams, symbols, energy, shadow beings.
Most moments —
I want to go back

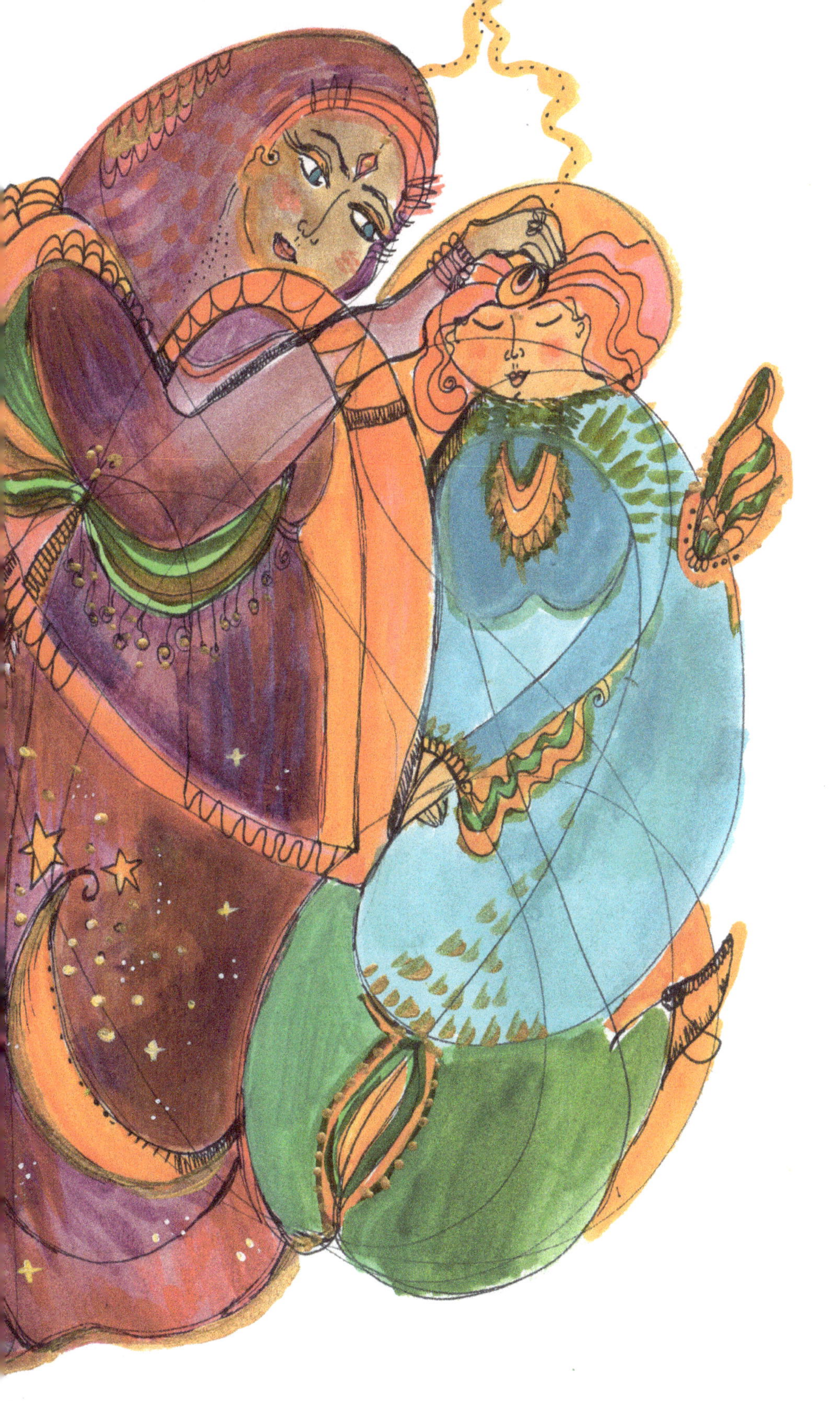

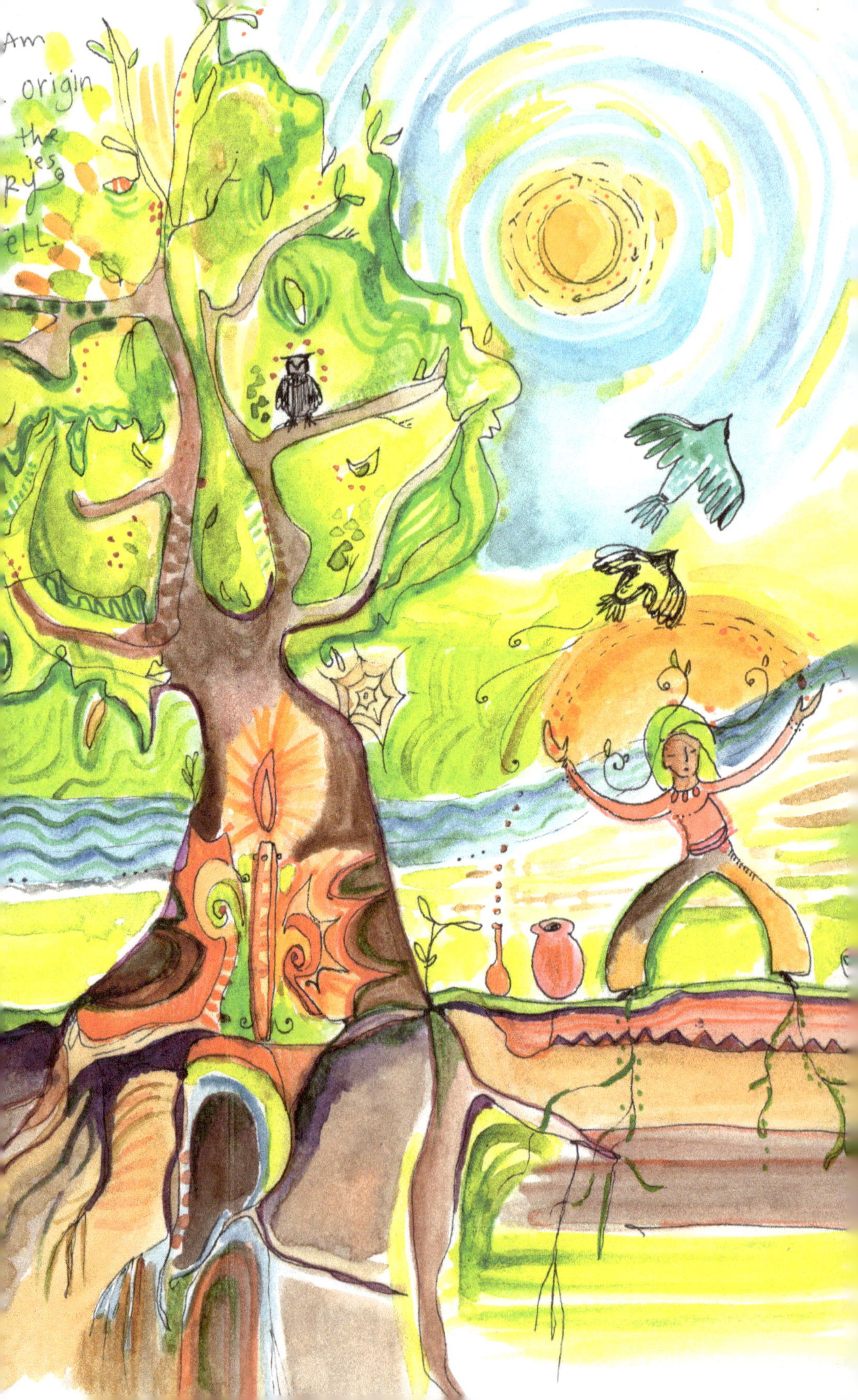
Am
origin
the
ies
ry
ell.

to how things were,
to black-and-white ease.
When all I had to do was arrive
and nod at another person's directions.
Who is 'I Am'?
Who is this Radical Love —
that urges me to look under rocks and behind trees?
The days of dogma are over.
I cannot simply stand and recite prayers of the Empire.
Sing songs to a King.
Because now I understand
that there were times before patriarchy –
when hieroglyphics were honored,
when women wrote on cave walls,
when people danced in circles,
when women's hands played drums,
when mama's breasts were full of reverence,
when holy clay held ancient consciousness.
Now I know:
the Father let me go
to be a voice for the Mother.
And there is no turning back.

WILD WOMAN

Wild woman,
I bare my feet
in the foam of the sea,
live on the creative cusp
where patterns pop
and whimsy whirs;
where breeze of Spirit
leads me to shadows,
squeezes my hand
while I make peace
with the beast within,
learn from the dragon,
befriend elementals,
call out to the angels.
Untamable,
I preach welcome for all,
even as I stumble
over my words.

I'm a student of mystery,
petition the mushrooms.
I stand with
my sacred rebel friends to
speak my true voice,
express my creative heart,
risk a new path.
We move forward,
together —
to shift the tide.

WHOLLY MADE

Beautiful soul –

Before you look into the eyes of another and say "I love you" (please),
    look into a mirror and gaze at your soul-filled windows and love yourself.

Before you go chasing down good looks and a long stride, (please)
    chase after the creative urges you have within and give them life.

Before you pen a love letter divulging all your honey's fantastic traits, (please)
    sit down with a fancy pen and proclaim the fabulous nature of you.

Before you tell your darling all the things that drive you crazy for them, (please)
    give yourself kudos for the unique pizazz you bring to your union.

Before you share all your secrets, hopes, dangerous truth, (please)
    tell yourself the whole truth and view yourself with no judgment.

Before you fill up with afternoon snuggles and give all your time away, (please)
    honor yourself with a regular rhythm of sweet solitude.

Before you convince yourself you are nothing without the other, (please)
    remember the daily grit you've endured to wade individual trials.

Before you give your body over to another's hands, (please)
    slow down and recognize your body for the sacred temple it is

Remember —
You are complete.
You are wonderfully and wholly made —
as you are.
Becoming. . .*you.* . .

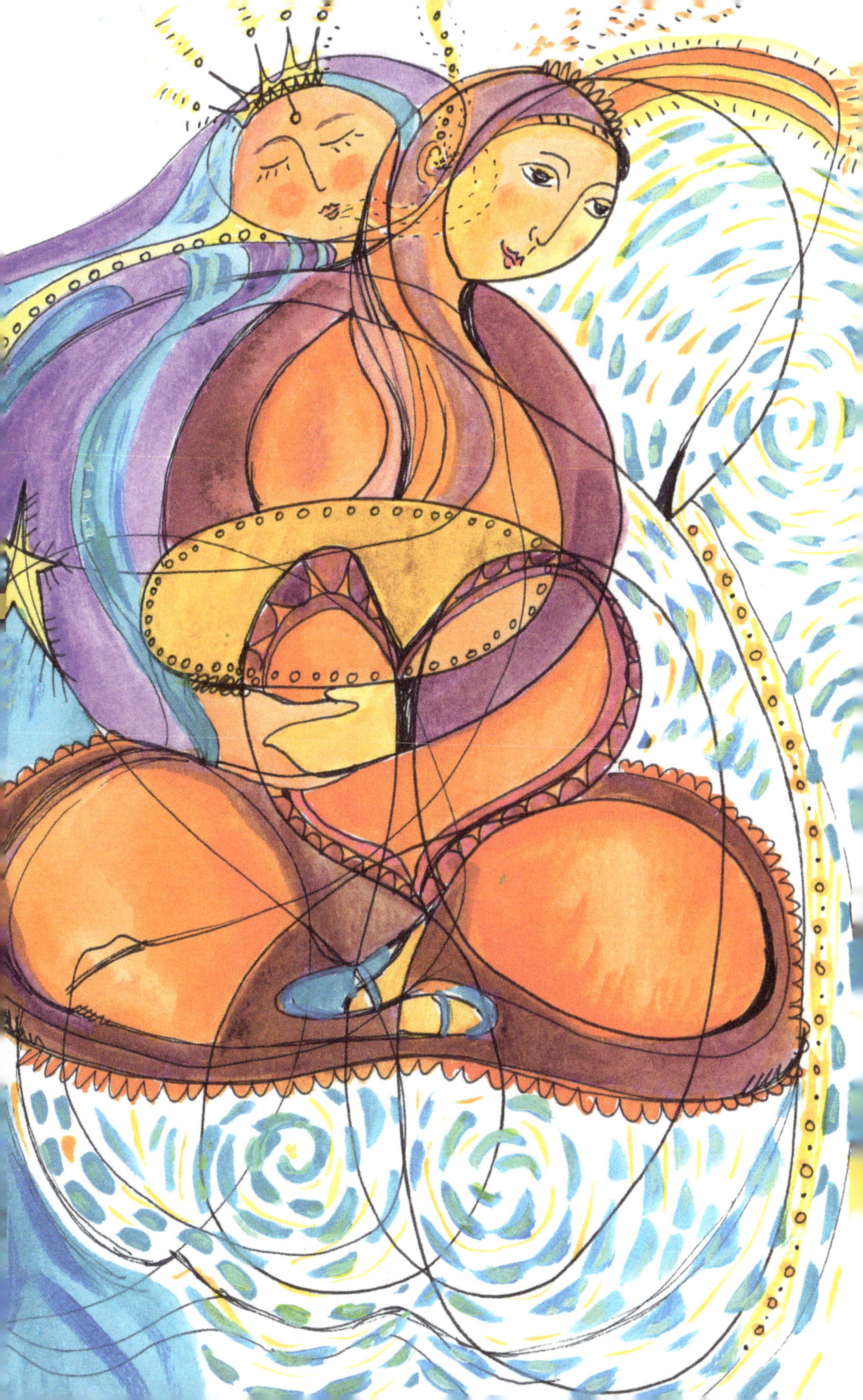

NOT ALONE

You don't go alone
with the wishes
in your soul.

You have another within you:

She, boundless Spirit —
present to your pulse,
skips with your heartbeat;

She, guardian helpmate —
holds your hand
for better or worse;

She, queen of your heart —
backbone to your cares,
prompts you to tend your life;

She, cadence of rest —
fills you with *I love you's,*
energizes your heart;

Together, you carry
the bread of life;

with her, you float
on the winds of love.

CALLED

You are the one
who holds the golden orb —
the power to love
with your words,
ignite hearts
with care.

There is no need
to advise, to
ramble on and on,
opinion after
opinion.

Simply
model
the
love
you
receive
from
MotherGod.

Embody it.

When you do,
your presence
becomes a calm welcome
to those in your midst.

Your healing energy
pulses in and through you
and carries you into the world
with peaceful insight.

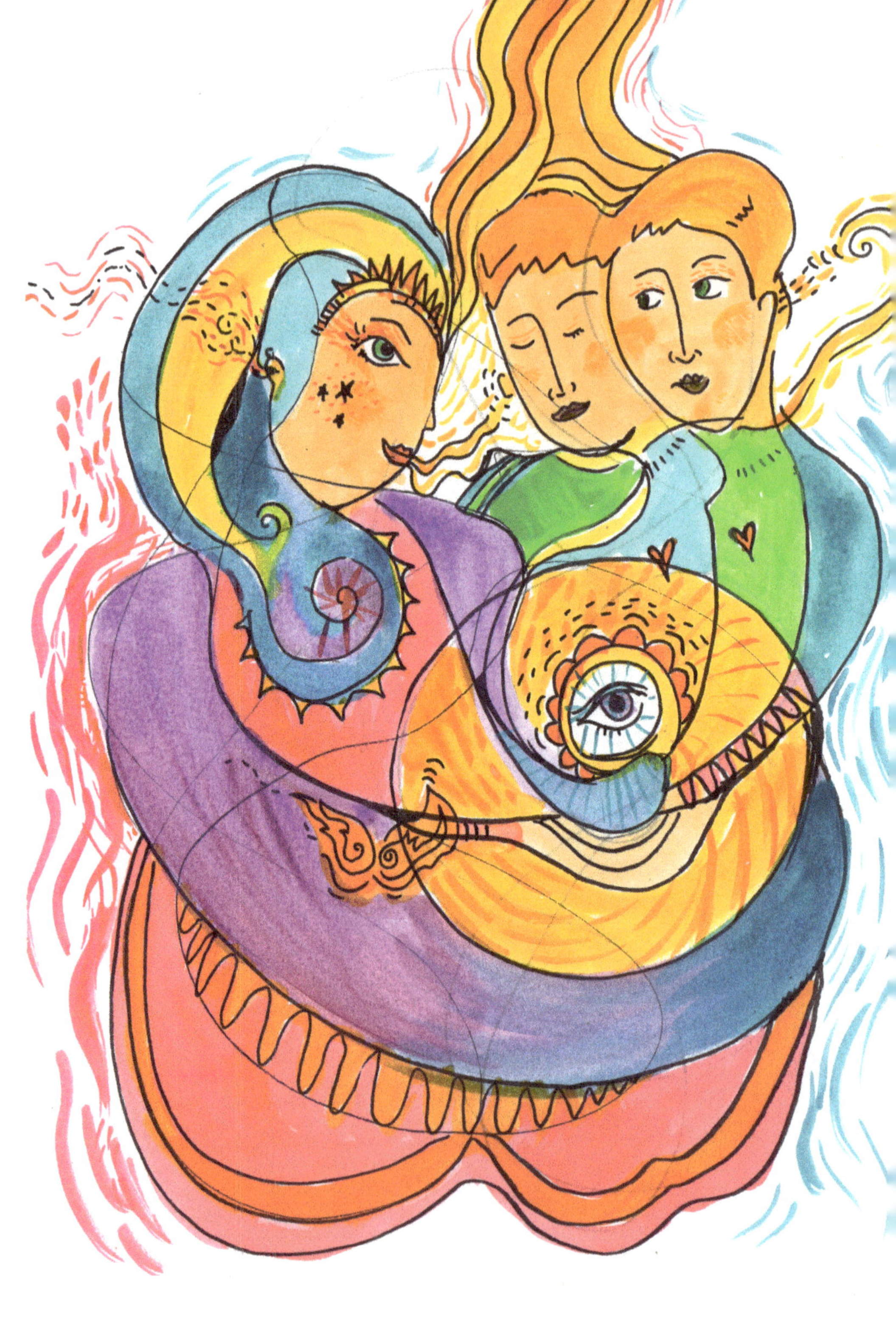

A POETIC REFLECTION ON *I AM SHE*

Dear Colorful You —

> *What is the shape of your power?*

> *What is the color of your grace?*

> *What is the texture of your beauty?*

> *What is the line of your fierce becoming?*

> *What is the pattern of your compassion?*

> *What is the symbol for MotherGod*
> *who lives within your bones?*

Draw it.
See it.
Receive it.
Declare it.

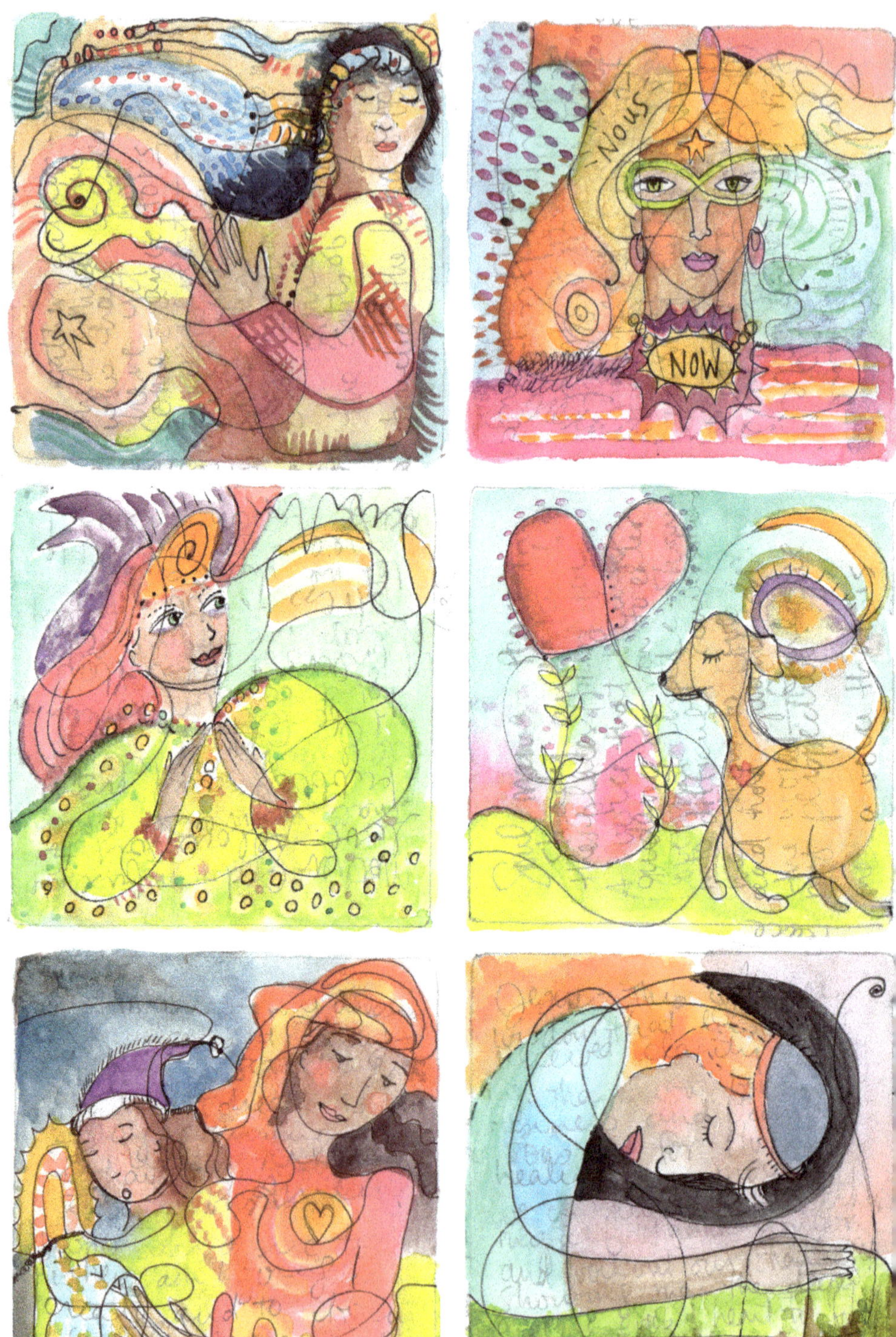
Nous
NOW

Prayer Squares Practice

A Journey to Visual Prayer

There was a time when I mightily struggled in my prayer life. I wondered what prayer was, why spoken prayer left me agitated and felt empty when I silently prayed. I knew in my heart that prayer extended beyond words and this notion prompted me to explore. Soon enough, little lights were showing up on my path. Doors opened and what I suspected was confirmed — prayer could be a movement, a stillness, a song, a swath of paint, a glorious thought, a way to gaze. Our very lives could be a living prayer — a communion with Divine Love. This confirmation led me to engage with my art as prayer. Aha! Art as prayer became an offering, a conversation, a moment-by-moment relationship. With great relief, the "perfect end product" was released as I explored my art as prayer. I discovered prayer is full of possibility and magic when it's a visual process of relationship with LOVE.

Prayer Squares Was Born

Prayer Squares took form at the onset of the pandemic in 2020 when I desired to share an intentional and visual way people could express their heartfelt needs, desires and sorrows. I was compelled to create a simple, visual prayer offering for individuals to hone in on love and healing as the pandemic spread and discord increased in our world. Since then, I've continued to shape, tweak and learn with this process.

So, What Is Prayer Squares?

Prayer Squares is a simple, 4-step spiritual practice for all ages to spark prayer life in a fun and fresh way! With a pencil, black permanent marker and color of your choice, Prayer Squares invites you to pour out, listen in and allow your inner Divine love to arise through word, line, color and reflection. What I love most about Prayer Squares is the surprise that occurs in only ten to fifteen minutes!

This practice can be engaged as a daily check-in or with a theme in heart. You can create your Prayer Square as an individual or invite a friend to join you. Or, it can be practiced in a wider circle as a family or community to create a communal vision of prayer. It's simple enough for small children all the way up to older generations — a great way to bring intergenerational community together.

- Pencil

- Black permanent marker

- White Paper or Sketchbook

- Watercolors, Markers or Colored Pencils

- 3"x 3" template made from cardboard

STEP ONE: PENCIL

First, trace your 3"x3" template to create a square on your page. Consider, "What prayer does my heart want to express?" Then, with your pencil, write down your prayer inside the square. Allow your words to flow naturally. Let it be a sentence, a short phrase or just one word.

STEP TWO: FREEFLOWING LINE

With your black permanent marker, release your prayer by making a free flowing line. Instead of controlling the outcome, allow your hand to guide you, follow where your pen wants to go. Draw your line without picking up your pen. Then, rotate your square and look at your line in different directions. Notice what you "see." What wants to be developed? You'll notice that my prayer is upside down because I see a heart shape and want to further play with that.

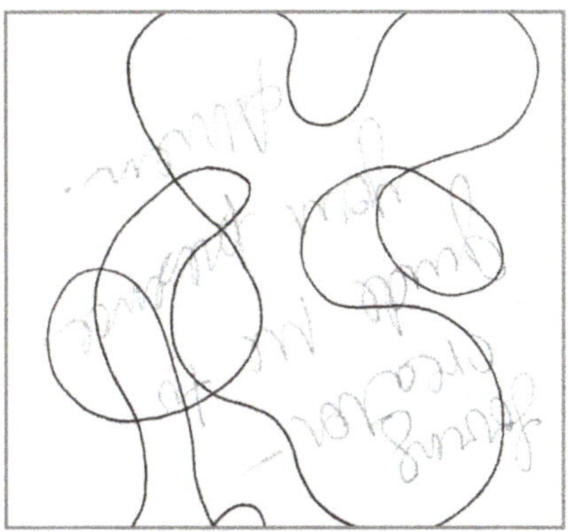

STEP THREE: DEVELOP IMAGE & ADD COLOR

Now, get playful and add more lines with your marker to your prayer. Add anything else that desires to be included. I often love to turn my lines into shapes, faces and animals. What color is your prayer? With watercolors, marker or colored pencil, take your time and color your prayer. Allow the color to express the hope of your prayer. Fully immerse yourself in the joyful nature of this step.

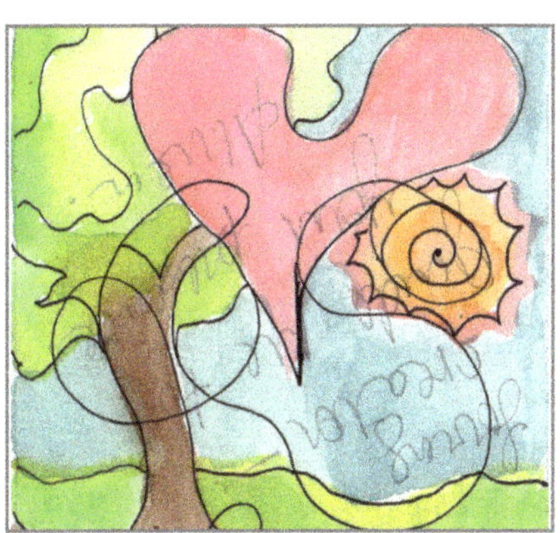

STEP FOUR: TEND & RECEIVE

Now, slow down and tend your creation. Feel free to add more color or make small marks to honor your image. BE with your prayer. As you engage, listen for the message of your prayer. What is it speaking to you? Along the edge (or back) of your square, write down what you glean. The message I received for the above prayer is "Love infuses nature."

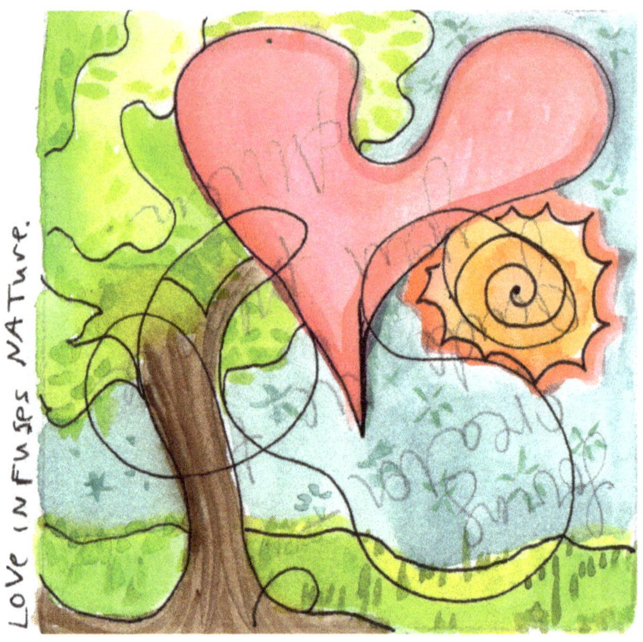

ACKNOWLEDGMENTS

"The soul is like a wild animal—tough, resilient, savvy, self-sufficient and yet exceedingly shy. If we want to see a wild animal, the last thing we should do is to go crashing through the woods, shouting for the creature to come out. But if we are willing to walk quietly into the woods and sit silently for an hour or two at the base of a tree, the creature we are waiting for may well emerge, and out of the corner of an eye we will catch a glimpse of the precious wildness we seek." — Parker J. Palmer, A Hidden Wholeness: The Journey Toward an Undivided Life

Since an early age, I've known my creations were connected deeply to my soul space. As a sensitive child, I inherently cradled my body over my art, my left arm curved around the paper as I drew with my right hand — protecting my images — my soul — from any type of danger that came in the form of careless commentary.

Part of my personal pilgrimage has been one of making friends with the still place to woo my wild artist soul out of hiding. The challenge has been discerning when to reveal this wooly wit of creative force to others. It has been a peculiar dance of risk taking — sometimes ending well, sometimes not. Still, each attempt of sharing image and word through a vulnerable approach has strengthened me.

By being heard and seen in quiet, caring spaces — places where love and listening were modeled — my heart (and soul) discovered belonging. Over time, I've been blessed by many who have fed me with spoonfuls of grace after I've expressed my creative truth. Each encounter has given me fresh kindling as I've followed the sacred, creative path.

Thank you to Wildhouse Publishing for seeing my vision and saying YES to a full color book that allows for people to slow down and engage their creative, sacred soul. Thank you to my editor, Mark Burrows, for being a truly gracious and enthusiastic guide breathing wind into my sails. You understood the depth of the whimsical images and offbeat poetry immediately. Your encouraging spirit and wise edits have been an immense gift to me.

Thank you to the facilitators and teachers of the Lifelong Learning Program at Columbia Theological Seminary; you craft embodied experiences of Divine Love. Your inclusion of creative reflection and intimate, contemplative circles of worship revisioned my idea of faithful spaces and set me on a path of transformation. Thank you to minister friends who have supported my exploration of art, word and faith, especially: Maggie Beamguard, Debra Weir, Ryan Bonfiglio, Denise Moore, Michael Moore, Elizabeth Doolin, Austin Vernon, John Hage, Rod Stone, and Roger Simmons. Also, thank you to Ken MacDonald — you are a model of love.

Thank you to artist, Shiloh Sophia, for teaching creativity and sacred story as an intentional way to keep love at the center. Your guidance of ritual, lineage, circle and conscious painting has brought me profound healing and the ability to move through the unknown easier. Thank you to the Musea community and the many women I've spent time in Red Thread Circle with — your authenticity has flourished my ability to witness, listen and speak my truth. Deep gratitude is extended to Jena Owen, Milagros Suriano-Riviera, Trish O'Malley, Natalie Moyes and the Red Madonna Sisterhood for carrying the torch of grace and love.

I'm grateful for a supportive network of wild women friends who stoke my creative fires. Thank you, Monica Hix, for walking with me for years as a spiritual companion and hearing my deep desire to turn this book into reality. Thank you, Sue Hudson, for diving fully into creative practice with me; your faithfulness as confidant, encourager and soul sister has been a nourishing well to drink from. Thank you, Penny O'Donnell, for your steady presence, life wisdom and generous way of listening. Thank you, Amy Loblaw, for welcoming *all of me* and *delighting* in exploring new terrains aside me. Thank you, Sophie Michaud, for traversing dream spaces and Mother havens with me; you are a dear companion of the dark. Thank you, Bobbie Boiselle, for bubbling with rainbows, Reiki and laughter in support of my creative work. Thank you, Megan Scott, for the way you ooze color, creativity and love; you are an inspiration. Thank you, Harmony Hicks, for speaking words of life into me since our friendship began; your heart is gold. To my late friend, Kristen Rietkerk — this book would not be here without you. Many years ago, when I had so much stirring inside me and not a spacious way to share it, you spoke the life-giving words to me, "Start a blog." And, I did.

Thank you for the sparks along my path who've shared wisdom for me to dwell upon: Jennifer Murray, Ellen Gadberry, Laura Satira, Sarah Van Sciver, Petra Rosenthal and Mary McCrystal. My gratitude runs deeply for the soulful, wise women who've joined me in-person or online to create. It has been an honor to grow our wings and fly together. My heart overflows in gratitude to Ruth Anna Abigail, Charlene Kinelski, Emily McCollum, Laura Murdock, Susan Rogers, Ann Woodfield and Elena Urzi. Your willingness to consistently show up to yourselves as sacred creators and BE with me in creative community has meant the world. Thank you, Laura Gingerich, for capturing the essence of my heart through your camera lens.

For the many people in my life who've given me words of encouragement about my spiritual walk, art and writing — thank you. Over time, all those notes, comments and kindness added up to keep my inspiration going. I'm humbled by the many artists, poets, contemplatives, and spiritual Wisdom teachers, living and beyond, who've gone before me, leaving their words and lives as an aroma of love for me to follow. Your teaching guides my way.

I'm grateful for my extended family who have witnessed and loved me through many phases and pursuits of a creative life. Pat and John Markotich, thank you for your ongoing love, interest and excitement at each step along my path. To my nieces, Abigail Lloyd and Katelyn Fridmann, thank you for your genuine curiosity of spiritual and artistic practice; I love witnessing both of you bloom into your brilliant becoming. To my sisters, Suzanne Fridmann and Kathryn Magee, you have been my teachers and advocates since day one. Thank you for your unwavering support of my art and writing. Your friendship, love and loyalty are threaded deeply within my heart. To my late mother, Mary Heitzman, and my father, Paul Heitzman, thank you for taking me to church, a sacred place that introduced me to "the mystery of faith" and let me grow and wrestle with the deeper questions of life. I'm beyond grateful you honored the arts in our home by modeling a love of music, artisanship and appreciation for beauty; your attention to detail made all the difference. Thank you for giving me ample opportunities to learn and expand my love of creativity. I love you.

In 2017, when I was at a crossroads in my life and chose to take my creative soul-self seriously, my family was my soft place to land. From the first timid strokes on a thin canvas, YOU were the ones who witnessed my trepidation and, still, celebrated my colorful marks. Lucas, you are full of compassion, heart and wit. Thank you for making me laugh daily and encouraging play. You teach me to be present to love, song and tenderness. Joshua, you see the world in a deep, vibrant, wide way. Thank you for soulful conversations that challenge me to stretch my perspective and further my understanding. You teach me to seek discomfort and say, "YES!" to the moment. Chris, thank you for partnering with me to live a life of meaning and purpose and for being my number one playmate. Your consistent love, support and listening has given me courage to open the door to my true colors. You ground me with your steadfast love. Each one of you has inspired my art, my words, my desire to grow into a fuller version of myself. I love you.

Finally, to my readers: thank you for being curious about yourself as a soulful creator and supporting my work by buying a copy of this book. I wish you profound blessings and encouragement to listen to the still, small voice within yourself. May you live connected to your colorful zest, knowing fully that you are loved and embraced by MotherGod.

Image Index

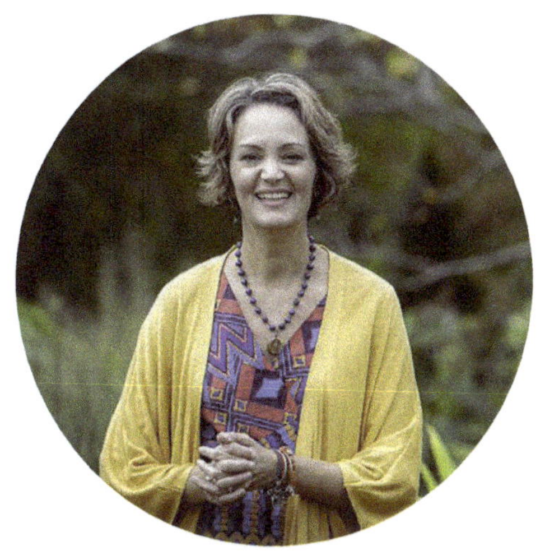

About Ally

Ally Markotich is an artist, poet, and Creative Formation Practitioner. She is the creator of Soul Kindling LLC, an online creative website where she offers courses and private sessions for people to spark their sacred imagination, open prayerful possibilities and nurture feminine intuition through color, drawing, and the magic of words. Ally is certified as a Red Thread Guide and Intentional Creativity® Educator from Musea under the guidance of artist, Shiloh Sophia. She is certified in Spiritual Formation from Columbia Theological Seminary and is a Holy Fire Karuna Reiki® Master in the tradition of Mikao Usui. She graduated with a BFA (Graphic Design) from Alfred University and lives in the Piedmont of North Carolina with her husband, two sons and yellow lab. On any given day, you may find Ally out and about searching for shiny truth, good books, and ice cream. You can find more of her art, musings and offerings at soulkindling.com.

Photo credit © Laura Gngerich

www.ingramcontent.com/pod-product-compliance
Lightning Source LLC
Chambersburg PA
CBHW050029040726
47599CB00015B/1597